MW00953792

When Death Is NOT Theoretical:

The Readiness of the Music Group 'Queen' for Living with Freddie Mercury's Dying

[2nd edition – with an Addendum & now an Index; overall 40% longer than the 1st edition]

Robert Charles Powell

Enjoy!
C Powell
2020

Once you accept fully into your being
that you can die, that you will die,
that you might be dying right now
you never go back.[1]

2

Addendum for the 2nd edition – page 61
Index – page 72

North Charleston, SC: CreateSpace Independent Publishing Platform, 2018
Copyright © 2018
Robert Charles Powell

ISBN-10: 1984909495
ISBN-13: 978-1984909497
Second Edition: January 2018
10 9 8 7 6 5 4 3 2 1

Code of Best Practices in Fair Use for Scholarly Research in Communication
http://cmsimpact.org/code/code-best-practices-fair-use-scholarly-research-communication/
Report by The International Communication Association; June 2010
The Center for Media & Social Impact http://cmsimpact.org/codes-of-best-practices/
School of Communication, American University, Washington, DC

Several recent lists of North American funeral songs include the "classic rock" anthems "You're My Best Friend!" and "Another One Bites the Dust!" – the first one recommended, the second one strongly discouraged. Our English-speaking cousins to the east and the west increasingly favor "Who Wants to Live Forever?" and "The Show Must Go On!" While a wide variety of contemporary tunes are showing up on these lists, these four particular "hymns" share the same source: the British music group "Queen". No other music group demonstrates this kind of clustering on the lists.[3] During the last decade each of these four specific recordings has been re-released by Queen at least twice in North America – not to mention at least seven times in the overall English-speaking world – and multiple vocalists have released their own versions. Three of these four songs were featured at least six times – and two at least seven times – over the last decade on the popular television programs, "American Idol," "Canadian Idol," and "Glee". The presentation of the "Global Icon Award" in 2011 featured a rendition of the increasingly most popular of these four songs, "The Show Must Go On!" – a defiantly mellow song that can be embraced by those who are grieving:

Inside my heart is breaking ....
I have to find the will to carry on! [4]

That is, members of the "Baby Boom" generation, now old enough to be faced more frequently with death than earlier in their lives, feel free to choose from an array of songs beyond "Amazing Grace," but they have been tending to look especially to one music group – Queen – as a source of funeral songs – if they are open to pondering death at all.

"Someday I will die" is about as much as most people are willing to admit – and they would rather not think much further about it. For most

3

people, at least in North America, and probably in Europe, that they will die is something "theoretical". The more people one knows, and the longer one lives, the more likely one will be aware of others' dying – but that is not the same as being aware of one's own dying, which actually has been going on since birth. Even those who have experienced "close calls" – who have brushed against death because of acute illness or an accident – are quick to put all thoughts of death out of mind. "Life is for the living. Death is for the dead," so they think.[5] But, what about those who live every day with death as an integral part of life? For some, death is not theoretical.

After some introductory remarks delineating the realm of life in which "death is not theoretical," this essay will home in on one specific example, the end of life of "Freddie Mercury" – born "Farok Bomi Bulsara" in 1946 – the extraordinarily talented frontman of the versatile music group Queen.[6] The focus, including theological overtones, will be on three aspects:

(1) the apparently seven-year period, from mid 1984 to late 1991, when Mercury actively dealt with dying while performing,

(2) the thirteen-year period before that when Queen already handled the double theme of "facing death head-on" and of "affirming life while fully aware of death", plus

(3) the effect of this very public dying and this persistent, quiet awareness of death both on Mercury's bandmates and on the group's fans as they became faced with death.[7]

This essay developed when I began pondering what it must have been like for Mercury's fellow musicians – Brian May, Roger Taylor, and John Deacon – first to grasp that something was amiss but not know what, then to learn that their frontman's illness was terminal. The members of Queen agreed not to discuss the upcoming death at all, as per Mercury's request, but to use the remaining time to write and to perform as much music as they could. There is no one right way to handle "living with dying," but this one specific example demonstrated one approach to a very public departure.

4

A Typology of Death.

I have a rendezvous with Death ....[8]

One can slice and dice a topic any number of ways.[9] This essay will concern primarily the reactions to "death from a disease with a somewhat known, non-immediate time-course," which, psychologically, is somewhat similar, actually, to "death from a weapon in a war-zone". Both of these kinds of death, before they happen, are not at all theoretical to the persons involved. They see the reality of death quite clearly on the near horizon. This essay will not primarily concern "death from 'natural causes' " or "death from car crash, murder, or natural disaster". Both of these latter kinds of death, before they happen, are somewhat theoretical to the persons involved. They see possibility of death quite vaguely on the far horizon. A key difference between the former two situations – when death is not theoretical – and the latter two situations – when death is theoretical – is the amount of incentive and time one has for thinking and re-thinking about the reality of demise – an obsessing for which most of us are hard-pressed to find words.

Everyone knows that death will come somehow, someday, but those experiencing more average or accidental deaths are less inclined to ponder the situation than those experiencing war-zone danger or dire prognosis. These latter people are very aware of death, and they view death as something clearly possible in a foreseeable future. Overall, for most Judeo-Christian Euro-Americans, this is an "abnormal" way of living – and there is much out of the ordinary about it before death occurs – so this is a type of life not readily discussable with those not in a similar situation. For

5

these people, "dying" and "living" inhabit one universe of thought. The "shadow of death" touches the "light of life". Death seems to be part of everyday living, and the reality of death is factored into how one lives one's life. The future seems determined and not everything seems possible, as one knows what is coming one's way. These people are impelled toward learning to accept death. In some other places and some other times this indeed has been the norm. There is stigma associated with these people and the upcoming deaths in their lives. They have had to experience others not sharing their reality as hesitating to begin relationships with them. They have had reason to think of keeping their upcoming deaths private lest "social death" come first. These people make special effort to avoid death, especially a non-laudable death, and living longer is necessarily a conscious goal.

For those destined for "death from a weapon in a war-zone," death is violent and sudden in coming, with an anticipated likely time, and it is more likely to make the headlines. This is an uncertain, somewhat non-time-bound, relatively-risk-taking-related death. There is considerable room for choice in this living or dying according to one's own actions. In contrast, for those destined for "death from a disease with a somewhat known, non-immediate time course," death is non-violent, slow in coming, with an anticipated likely time, and it is less likely to make the headlines. This "dire prognosis" death is a certain, somewhat time-bound, relatively non-risk-taking-related death. There is some – but not much – room for choice in this living or dying not according to one's own actions.

Death from a Disease with a
Somewhat Known, Non-Immediate Time Course.

*Now, this valley [of the shadow of death] is
a very solitary place.*[10]

Let us explore this one variety of death in some greater detail. People dying slowly, for example, of acquired immune deficiency syndrome – "AIDS" – including its complications, or from other slowly progressive "terminal" illnesses, such as some types of cancer, are very aware of death, and they view death as something clearly possible in a foreseeable future. In some ways it is easier to deal with a certain death that has a definite time-frame – death tomorrow or the day after – than with a certain death that keeps one guessing – especially if the supposed dire prognosis for the illness is not as "carved in stone" as some would like to suggest. People dying in "about ten years" or even "about six months" are hesitant to say much to most others – "Why 'dampen the party'?" – and those around them do not want to go through "about ten years" or even "about six months" of a "death watch" either. The person with such a prognosis knows at some level that "about ten years" or "about six months" could mean almost anything but focuses on "ten years" or "six months" just to have some facsimile of certainty. If the person is younger, then others might have some sympathy, but if the person is older, then others might have a lot less sympathy, about someone getting to live "only" until seventy, for example, instead of until their otherwise expected span of life. In any case it is harder for others to sympathize with someone who will be around another ten years or even another six months than with someone who will be around another few days. Obviously, the focus here is not on "about ten years" or even "about six months" but on the notion of probable certain death in a foreseeable span of time – a span of time during which one is trying to live while actively dying. Certainly there are some who might blurt out to any and all, "I'm dying in about ten years" or "in about six months" but the more circumspect recognize that this is not information to be shared too far in advance with many or even anyone. A common reaction to such an announcement would be some degree of confusion – as in, "Do you want me to relate to you as someone who is living? or as someone who is dying?" One cannot have it both ways, so the person having a disease with a somewhat known, non-immediate time course frequently ends up keeping that information private until death becomes more imminent.

Overall, this dealing with probable certain death on an uncertain schedule indeed is, one would like to hope, an "abnormal" way of living. How do such people make any plans? Well, they do end up making plans, but with acknowledged or unacknowledged contingencies. "If the disease has not begun to show too much …." "If I'm still able to fight off most infections …." "If I've not become too anemic and fatigued …." "If doctors will be available just in case …." "If …." "If …." "If …." Most others probably are unaware of the internal monologues such people entertain constantly about the future. Even mundane decisions like whether or not to buy a "life-time" membership or to take out a "fifteen-year mortgage" suddenly take on new dimensions. Important decisions like whether or not to date or marry or have children suddenly take on even greater moral depth.[11]

For these people, their sense of the *quality* of life changes. It is a bit hard to be light-hearted while choosing a cemetery. Everything about life gets recalibrated. Instead of mentally comparing lives against those who died at the previously expected span of life, they begin comparing lives against those who died at whatever is the new expected death date. What was planned to be done in the future – an envisioned future that probably will not happen – is removed from the equation.

For these people, their sense of the *quantity* of life changes. Most people, if you ask them, have a vague idea of how long they think they and their loved ones probably will live – perhaps just by taking into account how long people in the respective families tend to live. They might not have thought much about it, but certain notions of longevity are part of their identities. When a disease with a somewhat known, non-immediate time course comes along, these people suddenly have to rearrange their entire views of longevity. "Oh, I guess that novel that was going to be finished in retirement isn't" – because the life at hand no longer reaches that far. A Jew might say the common prayer, "*Shehekianu*," and pause at the last line – "enabled us to reach this day" – realizing that there will be a lot fewer days to come – while also realizing the blessing it has been to make it this far. That both the quality and the quantity of life have changed all at once can feel quite confusing.[12]

Let's face it: how many people want to start an intimate relationship or a high-stakes business partnership with someone whose death is quite foreseeable? How many people want to be referred to a personal physician or attorney who might not be alive when needed? How many people can accept attendance at a funeral upon first meeting someone? Those who deal with death all of the time might be able to handle this, but most normal mortals steer clear. For that matter, how many of those with a disease with a somewhat known, non-immediate time course can comfortably embark on new social engagements without having at least a passing thought about the emotional complications this might induce? So, these people possibly stick with understanding friends from the past, meet those similarly situated, or at least slightly socially withdraw. Not sharing with others this newly large part of one's life is preferable to being rejected. There is quiet aloneness in the shadow of death.

As Samuel Johnson once put it, "when a man knows he is to be hanged in a fortnight, it concentrates his mind wonderfully".[13] Others might think about how they will die – but then they might not. Those who can see death "on the calendar," however, definitely tend to think through the limited options. Are there embarrassing scenes to avoid? Are there overdue changes to embrace? In this living or dying not according to one's own actions, there is little room for choice – but there might be some room. Becoming a "victim" suits certain people. Becoming a "hero" suits others. Ignoring the whole situation is yet another option – dying exactly as one was living. The notion of choice is, however, front and center.

The Music Group "Queen"

**A Persistent, Relatively Non-Morbid
Concern with Death –
mid 1971 to mid 1984;
Staying Alert/ Standing Fast;
Maintaining Life/ Vanquishing Evil;
Accepting the Responsibility to Live before Dying.**

> *We believe in fighting evil
> by enjoying an abundant life ....*[14]

One of the most curious aspects of Queen's music is that this music group – Queen was a lot more than just "a rock and roll band" – was singing about death and various theological themes from the very beginning, with little if any comment about this by contemporary critics.[15] This is not an argument that can be made with great statistical rigor. The point is just that most popular music groups in the period mid 1971 to mid 1984 were not performing such songs on such a persistent basis – especially without being overly morbid, "Gothic," rebellious, or anti-war. Furthermore, when Queen was not focusing on what it means to die, it persistently admonished fans to go out and "Live!" The meanings of many of the songs are somewhat ambiguous – many of them could be viewed as "love songs" – but after a while it becomes untenable to use that excuse; most music groups do not have numerous possible "love songs" that however ambiguously seem to concern death.[16] For that matter, most music groups do not have so many songs admonishing people to stay alive.[17]

Queen's much re-recorded anthem "Keep Yourself Alive!" constituted, as one author noted, "a declaration of war against evil" – a comment that makes sense only if one grasps that Mercury, at least, viewed fighting death, evil, and negativity as a mandate that can be fulfilled only by staying very much alive.[18] Take a look at any of the many lists of "the top one hundred" popular songs of the 1970s, and about the only songs even closely comparable are "Stairway to Heaven" by "Led Zeppelin," "Stayin' Alive" by "The Bee Gees," and "I Will Survive" by Gloria Gaynor. During that same decade Queen performed no less than thirteen songs somehow relating to death and its defiance.

"Keep Yourself Alive!", by May, did not make much of a splash in the music world with its initial launch (1971) – or its wild revival in 1981 – or its final re-release in 1990 – but retrospectively it is clear that the song – consciously or unconsciously – meant a lot to Queen. The song appeared as their first album's first track and re-appeared as the flip side of a single of their last album's last track, "The Show Must Go On!" – the growing funeral favorite. That is, Queen, as a group, opened with a defiant anthem about the need to remain strong and it closed with a re-affirmation about the need to remain strong. "Keep Yourself Alive!" brackets the first nineteen of the twenty years that all four of the musicians performed together and its emphases recur in at least four other of their songs. Already in 1971 they insisted,

> Keep yourself alive!
> It'll take you all your time & money.
> Honey, you'll survive! [19]

Three years later "The Seven Seas of Rhye," by Mercury, asserted,

> I'll survive! [20]

Another two years later "Somebody to Love," by Mercury, vowed,

> I ... ain't gonna face no defeat! [21]

Two years after that "Dead on Time," by May, reminded,

> Got to KEEP YOURSELF ALIVE! [22]

– and, yes, those lyrics were placed by their author in capital letters on the album jacket. Already in 1976 "You're My Best Friend!" by Deacon, appreciated that *you make me live!* [23]

Five years after that "Soul Brother," by the four collectively, theologically announced that,

He can make you keep yourself alive! [24]

the only question being whether "He" referred to Jesus, G-d, *Mithra, Ahura Mazda,* or another divine figure. Furthermore, the song "Keep Yourself Alive!" – at the start of Queen's career together, in 1971 – advised holding one's ground,

stay right where you are! [25]

The song "Don't Try So Hard!", by Mercury – at the end of Queen's career together, in 1991 – again advised holding one's ground,

stay right where you are! [26]

Thus the admonitions to stay alert – "keep yourself alive!" – and to stand fast – "stay right where you are!" – were not some throw away lines, but rather reflected an integral part of Queen's entire body of music. A reasonable question is, "Why?" Available evidence suggests that John Deacon was and Roger Taylor became nominal Christians during these decades – but only four of Deacon's and three of Taylor's compositions clearly carried theological overtones. In contrast, while neither Brian May nor Freddie Mercury openly discussed their religions – nominally Christianity and *Zarathustrism* or *Zoroastrianism*, respectively – their compositions clearly carried theological overtones on a consistent basis. May was not one to proselytize. As a *Parsi* or *Parsee* – a member of the Indian rather than the Iranian Zarathustrian community – Mercury was not one to proselytize either, as generally one must be born into his religion.[27] There is no available evidence that May and Mercury discussed theology – especially the general compatibility of their two religious traditions – yet they must have had some kind of conscious or unconscious understanding, as the persistent theological grounding of Queen is all too obvious. How else can one explain that Mercury, a Parsi, wrote the triumphant ballad, "Jesus" (1973), that May wrote about the anti-Christ, and that Mercury wrote much about the devil? Surely those two, if not all four of the musicians, had to have at least minimally discussed writing, performing, and recording these songs – the theological implications of which the

13

critics mostly ignored. In a nutshell, two main tenets of Parsi-Zarathustrian ethics to which Mercury apparently adhered are (1) maintain life, and (2) vanquish evil – admonitions quite compatible with the Judeo-Christian ethics to which May apparently subscribed. They thus apparently shared a conviction, even if not discussed, that staying alert and standing fast supported their commitment to confronting death, evil, and negativity head-on wherever these might be found.

"Keep Yourself Alive!" was but the first of Queen's many songs providing explicit "moral" encouragement and guidance – with similar ones being "Fight from the Inside" (1977), "Spread Your Wings!" (1977), "Don't Try Suicide!" (1980), "Put Out the Fire!" [that is, don't kill others!] (1982), "Keep Passing the Open Windows!" [that is, don't kill yourself!] (1983), "Stop All the Fighting!" (1985), "Don't Lose Your Head!" (1986), and "Hang On In There!" (1989). Just as one has to wonder how Queen got by with singing about Jesus, the anti-Christ, and the devil, one has to wonder how they got by with dispensing such persistent moral commentary to thousands upon thousands of fans – with critics taking minimal if any notice. None of this was the norm for a popular music group in the 1970s and 1980s.[28]

A Persistent, Relatively Non-Morbid Concern with Death – mid 1971 to mid 1984; Embracing Life, the Good, the Positive through Free Will – and Embracing Truth as the Pathway to G-d.

> *even to the end of his life*
> *he'll bring a little love.*[29]

While much of Queen's repertoire, quite frankly, is melodically beautiful, one of their earliest concert staples, "Hangman" (1972), can only be described as "jolting". The song, by Mercury, established quite unambiguously his – and most likely May's – very early concern with the theme of staring down death and the corollary mandate to stay alive.

> *Now you say you're tired of living?*

asked the song.

> *Now you say you're afraid of dying?*

Well, that's too bad.

> *Hangman says he gonna let you go. ...*
> *Hangman says he wanna let you go.*[30]

Like it or not, implies the song, we have responsibilities in this world – we have a lot of living to do before dying.

To the degree that "Hangman" was simplistic and blunt, "The March of the Black Queen" (1974), by Mercury, was subtle and complex. Mercury, in "My Fairy King" (1973), already had sung of someone having

15

drained the color from my wings,
broken my fairy circle ring,

but these were taken as thrown away lines.[31] "Wings"? "Ring"? Whatever. The Parsi symbolism went unnoticed. Musically, "The March of the Black Queen" could not be ignored. As the only Queen song – and as one of the few of any songs – written with multiple simultaneous rhythms and meters – the full version, like "Bohemian Rhapsody" (1975) and "The Millionaire Waltz" (1976), was too complicated to be performed live, although a shorter version went well on stage.[32] One can try to ignore that the song dealt with the theme of facing death, evil, and negativity head-on, with a super-ego like "voice from behind" reminding us of our responsibilities,

Spread out your wings.
You are an angel.
Remember to deliver with
the speed of light
a little bit of love and joy.[33]

It is a bit hard to ignore, however, the song's curious phrasing,

In each ... soul lies a man –

which was the exact opposite of the more customary phrasing,

in each man lies a soul.

Once again, a reasonable question is, "Why?" "In each ... soul lies a man" might be seen as emphasizing the "down to earth" aspect of the spiritual ideal. The phrasing, however, probably, came from a literal, visual grasp of the "*faravahar*" or "*farohar*" or "*fravashi*" – a main Parsi symbol – which shows a circle or ring (symbolizing the individual's portion of the universal good, positive, living soul) with two wings of five feathers (symbolizing "the five senses"), with two legs (symbolizing "good and evil"), a balancing tail of three feathers (symbolizing "good thoughts, good words, good deeds"), plus a human figure (symbolizing "free will") standing inside of it.[34] That is, for the "winged circle ring" image that Mercury dropped into two songs, the full interpretative phrase would be,

in each soul lies a man or woman with
free will –

the free will to embrace life or death, good or evil, the positive or the negative.

Queen's first real hit, "The Seven Seas of Rhye" (1974), by Mercury, echoed the "Keep Yourself Alive!" encouragement of

Honey, you'll survive!

and added a boast,

> *I'll survive ...!*
> *I'll defy the laws of nature*
> *and come out alive!*[35]

"The Seven Seas" may be a somewhat academic reference to a book by that name of "experimental rhymes" collected by Anglo-Indian Rudyard Kipling – a book dedicated to "Bombay" (now Mumbai) – a book very likely encountered in a high school writing course by another Anglo-Indian, Mercury, who attended school near Mumbai and who certainly also favored experimenting with melodies and meters.[36] Another very real possibility, given the boast, "I'll defy the laws of nature," is that "The Seven Seas of Rhye" was a play on words – a veiled reference to the "seven rays" of "*psi*" – or "psychology" – a popular theory among some more mystical Parsis which concerned the seven "cosmic emanations of G-d" that guide personality – a theory which encouraged a positive, willful, defiant confrontation of evil and death.[37] In any case, this persistently popular song woke up a few with its lordly tone and its piano *arpeggios* played an octave apart.

"Bohemian Rhapsody" (1975), quickly followed by "The Millionaire Waltz" (1976) – both by Mercury – made it impossible not to notice the complexity – musically and symbolically – of Queen's songs, these two both flirting – one in a frightening manner and one in a flippant manner – with the denial of death. Queen refused to supply any interpretation of the more troublesome "Bo Rhap," as the six-minute masterpiece came to be known, although just about everyone agreed that the song's words had to mean "something". Yes, Queen still explored death, evil, and the negative, but with such a mixture of bluntness and beauty that listeners were – and still are – somewhat overwhelmed. The line "Hangman, hangman, waiting for me" arrested listeners' attention, but the line "Mama, 'just killed a man" in "Bo Rhap" really startled listeners –

and the song just kept on going, proceeding rapidly from a moralistic ballad to a layered guitar solo to operatic crescendo to unforgettable hard rock. Once listeners and the critics settled down, some began wondering, is this about homicide? or suicide? or abandoning a self? or good opposing evil? or what? Most, if they concluded anything, ended up viewing the song's arguing about death as reminiscent of a medieval morality play.

With "The March of the Black Queen" (1974) having made a play on images and "The Seven Seas of Rhye" (1974) having made a play on words, it is no wonder that "Bohemian Rhapsody," finished a year later, remains in many ways opaque. Nonetheless, "Bohemian Rhapsody" certainly drove home Mercury's and May's apparent message about the personal responsibility of living – of choosing "to vanquish evil" – even in oneself – before dying. The male narrator, though moaning in anguish,

> *I don't want to die!*
> *I sometimes wish I'd never been born*
> *at all!*

came to accept that there is

> *No escape from reality*

– that he had to

> *Look up to the skies and see*

– that he had to

> *face the TRUTH!*

– which was announced with dramatic finality in the song.[38] "The TRUTH" is a common loose translation of the Parsi concept of "*Asha*" – a notion also entwining the notions of purity and righteousness in reference to "the pathway to G-d" – a concept directly related linguistically to similar ones in Christianity and Hinduism.[39] Queen got by once again – this time in a big way – with leading unsuspecting listeners to contemplate some of the moral choices involved when facing death head-on.

A Persistent, Relatively Non-Morbid
Concern with Death –
mid 1971 to mid 1984;
Breaking Free and Breaking Through to
Shared Soul and to
Oneness with G-d at the End of Time.

> *all pride, all fear of embarrassment or failure –*
> *these things just fall away in the face of death ...*
> *Remembering that you are going to die is*
> *the best way ... to avoid the trap of*
> *thinking you have something to lose.* [40]

"You're My Best Friend!" (1975), by Deacon, the youngest and last musician to join the group, announced in a resigned but more positive manner – in a far more aesthetic manner than "Hangman" and a far more light-hearted manner than "Bo Rhap,"

> *you make me live!* [41]

Deacon, on at least some level, grasped the program seemingly being put in place by Mercury and May. This is reaffirmed by a composition he co-wrote with Mercury, "Spread Your Wings!" (1977), which appears to be another reference to the "faravahar" – the "winged circle ring" – and the soul's inherent free will:

> *Spread your wings ....*
> *Pull yourself together,*
> *'cause you know you should do better.*
> *That's because you're a free man.* [42]

19

Deacon got the gist of the Parsi "winged circle ring" – that one is free to choose a better and best path in life.

These encouraging expectations reappear in Mercury's "Keep Passing the Open Windows!" (1983), a song about avoiding suicide:

You just gotta be strong
and believe in yourself. ...
Oh, get yourself together! [43]

and in his "Mr. Bad Guy" (1985), overall reminding one of the freedom to escape a bad situation:

spread your wings
and fly away with me! [44]

"Somebody to Love" (1976), a continuing orchestral favorite by Mercury, combined a gospel structure with the commanding tone of "The Seven Seas of Rhye," proclaiming,

Ain't gonna face no defeat! [45]

Then the song echoed a line from "Bo Rhap,"

just got to get right out of here [46]

with the lines,

I just gotta get out of this prison cell!
Someday I'm gonna be free, Lord!

thus establishing yet another theological discussion that would carry through until Mercury's death.

The notion of "breaking free" or "breaking through" showed up over and over in Queen's lyrics. After appearing in "Bo Rhap" and "Somebody to Love," the notion came back in Deacon's "I Want to Break Free!" (1984),

Oh, how I want to break free! [47]

in Mercury and Taylor's "Breakthru" (1989):

Somehow
I have to make this final breakthru . . .
now! [48]

and in May's "The Show Must Go On!" (1991):

I'm aching to be free! [49]

This theme of "breaking free" drew upon the Parsi concept of "*frashokereti*" – of "making wonderful and excellent" – referring to the human soul's drive to become more and more pure until it finally can find release – break free from or break through – cycles of life and death – until it finally can become at one with G-d at "the end of time".

"Save Me!" (1979), by May, was one of the first of Queen's songs explicitly calling upon divine assistance with staying alert and standing fast:

> *Save me! Save me! Save me!*
> *I can't face this life alone!* [50]

Implicitly, though, the earlier, equally haunting melody, by Mercury, "Nevermore" (1974) likewise conjured up at least the sense of hoping for help:

> *There's no living in my life anymore.* [51]

"Beautiful Day" (1980), by Mercury, was more neutrally melancholic,

> *Sometimes I feel*
> *so sad, so sad, so bad, but*
> *no one's gonna stop me now!*
> *No one!*
> *It's hopeless, so hopeless to even try!* [52]

Earlier, similar phrasing in his "Don't Stop Me Now!" (1978) was more clearly hypomanic in its defiance. Then May weighed in with two up-lifting songs. The first one, "The Hero" (1980), seemed mildly defiant and only vaguely called upon divine assistance:

> *lift your head to the stars, and*
> *the world's for your taking. ...*
> *the continuation [of this path in life]*
> *is yours for the making.* [53]

The second one, "Flash" (1980) seemed somewhat triumphant, with definite theological overtones:

> *Flash! a-ah!*
> *Savior of the Universe! ...*
> *He'll save every one of us! ...*
> *He's a miracle! ...*

King of the impossible! ...
He'll save with a mighty hand ...! [54]

While the song may have been speaking of a divinity, May was quick to keep alert, steadfast, striving mortals in the loop:

'Just a man,
with a man's courage.
Nothing but a man ....
No one but the pure at heart
may find the Golden Grail!

Queen once again admonished mere mortals to stand strong and aim high, so as to maintain life, vanquish evil, and achieve some degree of salvation.

"Soul Brother," the only Queen song specifically bearing the names of all four bandmates, clearly conveyed a theological mandate:

He can make you keep yourself alive! [55]

As noted above, the only question was whether "He" referred to Jesus, G-d, *Mithra*, *Ahura Mazda*, or another divine figure. The title itself – "Soul Brother" – rather than being a trite reference to simple comradeship was a theological reference to their "shared soul" – their deep connection with each other and with the spiritual:

He's my soul, brother!
He's my best friend –
He's my champion – and
He will rock you, rock you, rock you,
'cause He's the
Savior of the Universe!
He can make you
keep yourself alive –
make yourself alive! ...
'cause He's somebody –
somebody – you can love!

Thus Queen appears collectively to have "signed on" to the whole developing constellation of theological ideas.

In "There Must Be More to Life than This!" (1983), Mercury made it clear that their task would not be easy:

> *There must be more to life,*
> *much more to life. ...*
> *than this!*[56]

In "Hammer to Fall" (1984), May continued the theme from the negative side:

> *Here we stand or here we fall.*
> *History won't care at all! ...*
> *We're just waiting*
> *for the hammer to fall!* [57]

underscoring that no "Thanks" was to be expected. In "It's a Hard Life!" (1984), Mercury continued the theme from the positive side:

> *Yes, it's a hard life,*
> *in a world that's filled with sorrow. ...*
> *It's a long hard fight,*
> *but I'll always live for tomorrow.*
> *I'll look back on myself and say:*
> *"I did it for love!"*

emphasizing that, with or without anyone's approval or appreciation, the responsibility – through free will – to embrace life or death, good or evil, the positive or the negative, cannot be rejected.[58]

Living with Death: Not Talking about It –
But Singing even More about It –
mid 1984 to late 1987;
Clues Not Appreciated.

We've not ... spoken about it at all, ...
that time is running out ....[59]

While Mercury died late in 1991, Queen released new songs featuring Mercury's distinctive voice through 1995. Prior to about mid 1984 Mercury and May wrote most of Queen's songs dealing with death in relationship to life, but Deacon after 1984 and Taylor after 1987 increasingly wrote such songs, too. Once again, this is not an argument that can be made with great statistical rigor. The fact remains that there still was little if any comment by contemporary critics about the themes in Queen's music even as the group's frontman was dying right before their eyes. Granted, hindsight tends to have more perspective than foresight, but the data were piling up year after year that something unspoken was going on. Retrospectively, visual signs of Mercury's illness can be seen in videos from as early as late 1985. Retrospectively, it becomes obvious that Queen's music videos became more animated – even manic – perhaps to conceal that Mercury himself was doing less of the prancing and dancing for which he was known, as he had developed unhealing lesions on his right leg and foot. Retrospectively, it becomes clear that Mercury's sudden sporting of a beard then wearing of thicker and thicker makeup was to camouflage lesions disfiguring his face. Retrospectively, it makes sense that even Deacon – "the quiet one" – had begun giving press interviews, while the marital problems of Taylor and May were allowed an unusual amount of diversionary attention by the group. Clearly they were making concerted efforts to protect Mercury from the press. There were rumors about Mercury's health, but Queen – individually and collectively – worked overtime putting out new songs, so that music remained the more important story. Besides, it was a rare music group in the 1970s and 1980s that stayed together more than five years. Queen had already outlasted "The Beatles" by a decade, so their years of productivity seemed to extend far into the future. Yet, year-by-year Queen kept producing even more songs somehow dealing with death in relationship to life.[60] Take a look at any of the many lists of "the top one hundred" popular songs of the 1980s, and songs even closely comparable are notably absent. During that same decade Queen performed no less than thirty songs somehow relating to death and its defiance. In 1990 and 1991 Queen recorded ten more (although three were not released until 1995), plus May recorded one more in 1992 just after Mercury's death. The grand total comes to fifty-four songs, over a fifth of those released in the two decades by the members of Queen.

"Teo Torriatte!" ("Let Us Cling Together!") (1977), by May and sung by Mercury in Japanese, was the first in the Queen repertoire that seemed somewhat ambiguous as to whether it was primarily a ballad about love or a ballad about death.

> When I'm gone,
> no need to wonder
> if I ever think of you. ...
> Though I'm gone,
> it's just as though I
> hold the flower that touches you. ...
> Oh, be strong! ...
> We're all – you're all –
> for all – for always![61]

"Love Me Like There's No Tomorrow!" (1984), by Mercury, raised that question again, especially once there were suggestions that Mercury was becoming ill – actually seeming more so in 1984 than in 1985 or 1986.

Tomorrow,
who knows just what's in store for me?
Anything can happen but we
only have
one more day together – just
one more day forever – so,
love me like there's no
tomorrow! ...
This is our last goodbye
and very soon it will be over, but
today just
love me like there's no
tomorrow! [62]

The amount of sorrow in each of these songs is palpable, surpassed possibly only by the tear-evoking, "Who Wants to Live Forever?" (1986), by May:

touch my tears with your lips.
Touch my world with your fingertips. ...
Forever is our today. [63]

That is, "Oh, be strong!" – for "there's no tomorrow".

In melody and theme, "Time" (1986), by "outsiders" but chosen by them to be sung by Mercury, fits very well with sentiments that were in May's "Son and Daughter" (1973):

Watching the time –
mustn't linger behind, [64]

and in May's "Dead on Time" (1978)

'Got to leave on time! [65]

"Time" carried the lines,

time is running out for us ....
Time waits for nobody.
Time won't wait for no one. [66]

Just as Mercury's "Life Is Real" (1982), written in response to a friend's murder, skirted around saying that "death is real," the phrase "Time waits

26

for no one" skirted around saying that "death waits for no one". Though he had not yet sought medical confirmation, Mercury knew he was dying.[67]

Already in "G-d is Heavy" (1984) Mercury had sighed just that,
> *G-d is heavy.*
> *G-d is heavy.*
> *G-d is heavy, G-d is heavy.*[68]

In "Made in Heaven" (1985/1995), said to be one of his favorite songs, Mercury rejected the notion of hard and fast fate.
> *"Made in heaven." "Made in heaven."*
> *"It was all meant to be."*
> *Yeah. ... That's what they say.*
> *"Can't you see?" ...*
> *"Made in heaven." "Made in heaven."*
> *That's what everybody says –*
> *everybody says to me. ...*
> *"Wait and see."*
> *"It was really meant to be."*
> *"So plain to see."*
> *Yeah, everybody, everybody,*
> *everybody tells me so.*
> *Yes, "it was plain to see."*
> *Yes, "it was meant to be."*
> *"Written in the stars." ...*[69]

It is not clear that others caught his sarcasm. Mercury was not buying any of this. "Made in Heaven" (1985/1995) speaks to the Parsi notion of the interaction between destiny – "*Bago Bakht*" or "share of fortune" – and free will – with emphasis generally being placed on free will, while acknowledging that the soul's previous progress did somewhat determine its current state. He accepted
> *taking my ride with destiny ....*
> *playing my role in history ....*

Mercury accepted that while his "share of fortune" had been shaped by the past it could be shaped further through his own free will – no matter how dire the situation.

I'm having to learn to pay the price.
They're turning me upside down.
'Waiting for possibilities.
'Don't see too many around. ...

He accepted that how one lives, how one dies was "yours for the making". Forget fate. Forget thinking that anyone can deduce what G-d "meant to be". As Queen noted in the opening of their song, "One Vision" (1985):

G-d works in mysterious ways,
mysterious ways.[70]

Notice that except for some earlier input by May, Mercury wrote most of Queen's songs between mid 1984 and late 1987 that touched upon death. During this period, Taylor's input is conspicuously absent, even though, historically, he had been Mercury's "buddy". Quite in contrast for this period are the contributions of Deacon and Mercury's new friend, the Iberian opera diva, Montserrat Caballé.

Living with Death: Not Talking about It –
But Singing even More about It –
mid 1984 to late 1987;
   Clues Appreciated.

As far as can be determined, Mercury, putting in stunning stage performances in 1985 and 1986, still had not told his colleagues in Queen about the magnitude of his illness – yet, on some level, at least one of them seems to have known. Deacon's "One Year of Love" (1986) went on record with the opinion that

> *Just one year of love*
> *is better than a lifetime alone!* [71]

In a solo project, "No Turning Back" (1986) he reminded himself:

> *'Gotta live before I die.* [72]

May, too, might have deduced that something was wrong. While the main lyrics of his "Gimme the Prize (Kurgan's Theme)" (1986) were not revealing, in the middle of the piece a gruff voice, for no apparent reason, said,

> *it's better to burn out*
> *than to fade away.* [73]

Once again, Deacon showed quietly that he got the message. With Mercury he also wrote "Friends Will Be Friends" (1986), reassuring that

> *When you're through with life*
> *and all hope is lost,*
> *hold out your hand, 'cause*
> *friends will be friends –*
> *right till the end.* [74]

Mercury acknowledged this, in a way, in the opening, haunting words that he wrote and sung in "Love Is the Hero" (1986), which was otherwise someone else's song:

> *Love is the hero ....*
> *Never say "never"!*
> *Never say "never"!*
> *Never say "never," say "never"!* [75]

Following this theme of loving support mixed with death defiance, Mercury produced some of the most beautiful music of his career in early 1987, just before he opened up, in confidence, to his bandmates. "La Japonaise" (1987), sung in Japanese and English with Caballé, who knew the truth of the situation, included the lines:

> *Trusting with no fears*
> *till the end.* [76]

"Barcelona" (1987), again sung with Caballé, promised,

> *if G-d is willing,*
> *we will meet again*
> *someday! ...*
> *cry, ... 'Come alive!' ...*
> *if G-d is willing –*
> *[we will be] friends until*
> *the end!* [77]

"Ensueño" (1987), with lyrics by Caballé sung by Mercury in Spanish, and reminiscent of "Teo Torriatte!" that Mercury had sung in Japanese, included, in English translation, the lines:

> *To come back to life.*
> *To know that my dream is not alone.*
> *It breathes in you.* [78]

These may well be love songs, but there is no getting around that Mercury probably also is singing of death. In his early 1987 meticulously prepared cover of "The Great Pretender" Mercury admitted,

> *Oh, yes, I'm the great pretender –*
> *pretending I'm doing well.* [79]

In a video-taped interview dated May 30, 1987, clearly visible on Mercury's left cheek is a so-called "[Moritz] Kaposi sarcoma" lesion – a frequent incidental finding associated with early acquired immune deficiency syndrome ("AIDS"). Deacon had had another "one year" with his close friend, and now wrote for him to sing "My Life Has Been Saved!" (1987). The original lines were blunt and sad enough:

> *I read it in the papers:*
> *there's death on every page.*
> *Oh, Lord – I thank the Lord above!*
> *My life has been saved!* [80]

but Mercury's recorded *ad lib* lines in 1989 chillingly spoke the truth of his situation:

> *I'm in no doubt.*
> *I'm blind.*
> *I don't know what's coming to me.*

"How Can I Go On?" (1987), by Mercury and Mike Moran, sadly asked,

> *is anybody there – to comfort me?*

then cried out,

> *Lord, take care of me!* [81]

"Headlong!" (1991), by May, captured another hint that Mercury struggled with the progression of his illness. In a slightly frantic tone quite different from any other of their compositions, the song admitted,

> *And you're rushing headlong –*
> *you've got a new goal!*
> *And you're rushing headlong –*
> *out of control!*
> *And you think you're so strong –*
> *but there ain't no stopping, and*
> *there's nothing you can do about it!* [82]

"Innuendo" (1991), co-written near the end with Taylor, included Mercury's brief, intrusive, somewhat desperate prayer, clearly addressed to G-d:

> *Destroy our fears!* [83]

31

By March 1991 Mercury definitely was half-blind, half-lame, extremely thin, and continually cold.

"Living or dying, we'll just keep on fighting!"
"We'll keep on tryin', till the end of time!" –
late 1987 to late 1991. [84]

> *there is a crown in death for him*
> *who strives well and perishes unstained ....*[85]

By late 1987 Mercury is said to have shared the confirmed diagnosis. Mercury specifically told May, Taylor, and Deacon that he did not want to talk about it further – that he did not want others to talk about it – that he wanted to make music until the end. Queen confronted the rumors with diversion and good offense, including the song, "Scandal!" (1989), by May and considered one of his favorites. The song certainly spoke for Mercury and somewhat spoke for the entire group:

> *it's just a private affair. ...*
> *and tell me, what do they care?...*
> *Today the headlines,*
> *tomorrow hard times ...*
> *and in the end the story*
> *deeper must hide –*
> *deeper and deeper and deeper inside.*[86]

Queen handled grief through their music.

Echoing "My Life Has Been Saved!" "Hang On In There!" (1989) by "Queen" celebrated their two more years together:

> *Don't let go! ...*
> *Thank G-d you're still alive! ...*

33

Hang on in there! [87]

"These are the Days of Our Lives" (1990), by Taylor, was yet another love song hinting at death:

> *these are the days of our lives.*
> *They've flown in*
> *the swiftness of time.*
> *These days are all gone now, but ...*
> *one thing's still true:*
> *when I look,*
> *and I find:*
> *I still love you!* [88]

So was the beautiful instrumental piece, "Bijou" (1991), by May and Mercury, which had only a very few words at the end:

> *You and me –*
> *we are destined,*
> *you'll agree,*
> *to spend the rest of our lives,*
> *with each other –*
> *the rest of our days,*
> *like two lovers,*
> *forever.*
> *Yeah, forever,*
> *my bijou.* [89]

"Days of our lives" is a somewhat ancient phrase with an introspective ring about it – a phrase that can be taken as looking back toward the beginning – or as looking forward toward the end – or as both. In terms of looking forward, both "La Japonaise" and "Barcelona" spoke bluntly of till "the end". Similarly, "Innuendo" spoke of "till the end of time" and "Bijou" spoke of "the rest of our days". The focus on "the end" – "the end of time" – "the rest of our days" – occurs frequently in Parsi-Zarathustrian as well as in Judeo-Christian writings, and is implied in the Parsi concept mentioned above of "*frashokereti*" – of "making wonderful, excellent" – of driving toward purity by breaking away and breaking through to ultimate oneness with G-d. [90]

Oneness, as a concept, filled the blockbuster song "One Vision!" (1985) – released at the peak of Queen's career:

> One heart! One soul! ...
> One G-d! One vision! ...
> One flesh! One bone! ...
> One voice! One hope!
> One real decision! ...
> Gimme one vision! ...
> No wrong! No right!
> I'm gonna tell you
> there's no black and no white!
> No blood! No stain!
> All we need is one
> world-wide vision! [91]

Taylor re-opened the mantra a year later, with a hint of theological concern, in "A Kind of Magic" (1986):

> One dream! One soul!
> One prize! One goal!
> One golden glance –
> of what should be! ...
> One flash of light
> that shows the way! [92]

Mercury had the last words, sending an explicit theological message, in "All G-d's People" (1987/1991):

> So all you people,
> give freely!
> Make welcome
> inside your homes!
> Thank G-d, you people!
> Give freely!
> Don't turn your back on
> the lesson of the Lord! ...
> Rule with your heart and
> live with your conscience! ...
> Let us be thankful!

He's so incredible! [93]

Ancient Parsi texts emphasize the wisdom that comes truly from the heart and the faith – *"Daênâ Vanguhi"* – that comes from "good conscience". Thus, for one last time, Mercury and Queen got by with carrying a moral message to thousands upon thousands.

Not that many weeks before dying, Mercury composed, played, and sang the last song that was entirely his own, an unusually mellow ballad – "A Winter's Tale" (1991/1995) – a kind of taking leave of this world:

> *So quiet and peaceful –*
> *tranquil and blissful –*
> *there's a kind of magic in the air. ...*
> *It's all so beautiful ... .*
> *It's unbelievable.* [94]

Then Mercury's voice left him, just after his soulful singing of the first verse of his very last song, "Mother Love" (1991/1995), a song that revisited "Goin' Back", a cover he had released twenty years earlier. May, who wrote the song in Mercury's presence, had to finish singing it for the Queen frontman who was too ill to carry on:

> *I don't want pity,*
> *just a safe place to hide.*
> *Mama, please,*
> *let me back inside! ...*
> *'Got such a feeling*
> *as the sun goes down –*
> *I'm coming home to*
> *my sweet, Mother love.* [95]

Mercury, whose time had arrived for rebirth or renovation, believed that life "ends, as it began".[96] Mercury's, May's, Deacon's, and Taylor's two decades together were summarized – in song, of course – by May just after Mercury's death:

> *Living or dying,*
> *we'll just keep on fighting ...!* [97]

Ironically, without the early and pervasive theological influence of Farok Bomi Bulsara (1946-1991) – "Freddy Mercury" – the music group Queen might not have been ready to cope with the years during which their frontman was quietly, actively dying. For Queen, death was not theoretical.

Recapitulation:
When Death is Not Theoretical:
Lessons Learned from
Queen's Readiness across Seven Years for
Their Frontman's Death.

> *from all this gloom*
> *life can start anew*
> *and there'll be no crying soon.*[98]

    "Goin' Back" to their roots, appreciating anew the depths of their "One Vision!" that matured across twenty years, Queen accepted the reality of death in the midst of living.[99] Granting that "the end" lay closer than they had expected, the members of Queen lovingly supported each other in their defiance of the adverse circumstance that came their way, producing an immense body of work in their final seven years together, and allowing four more years for further closure.[100]

    While from the beginning Queen – especially Mercury and May – consciously or unconsciously – wrote about confronting death head-on, during their final decade together the group produced a number of songs that may well become classic resources in dealing with death and dying. Even just a few lines from Mercury's "Love Me Like There's No Tomorrow!" (1984) are worth a second look:

> *Tomorrow,*
> *G-d knows just where I'll be. ... so*
> *love me like there's no*

tomorrow!
Hold me in your arms,
tell me you mean it! [101]

The whole song conveys acceptance of a sweet anguish – an honest acceptance that "tomorrow" one might not be alive. Likewise, even just a few lines from Taylor's "These Are the Days of Our Lives" (1991) are worth savoring:

Those were the days of our lives.
The bad things in life were so few.[102]

The whole song – but this excerpt especially – conveys an acceptance that yesterday "was what it was" – that, there's "No Turning Back"– "Look straight ahead!"[103] Yes, "just keep on fighting," but there comes a time to let go of life – of living with dying – and move on into death.[104]

Mercury, at the very end, stated clearly what had been his unspoken stance: "I don't want pity". A year earlier he, with the group's support, announced, however shakily, his defiance of any attempt to define him by an illness:

Inside my heart is breaking...,
but my smile ... stays on! ...
I'm never giving in! ...
I'll top the bill!
I'll overkill!
I have to find the will to carry on! ...
The show must go on! [105]

And overkill he did. While his voice had become a bit ragged at the end of Queen's touring in 1986, many observers have commented on the increasing beauty of Mercury's voice between 1987 and his death four years later. He gave living while dying his all – and left life at the top. Mercury had no intention of being remembered just for dying. He refused to be defined by his illness or to be defined as a patient. That was his choice – and he recognized that others were free to choose a different path. While acknowledging destiny shaped by past actions, Mercury emphasized free will shaping present actions, and he said so straightforwardly in the lyrical bridge he inserted into "Innuendo" (1991):

39

You can be
anything you want to be!
Just turn yourself into anything you
think that you could ever be! [106]

Mercury believed that death, like "life, is real"– and that death, like "time, waits for no one".[107] Queen played what turned out to be its last public concert in August 1986 – with all 120,000 tickets sold-out within two hours – and then the members took a break from each other to work on their own projects – until that phase stopped abruptly in September 1987. Between January 1988 and June 1991 they spent an immense amount of time in the recording studios. Mercury was the one dying, but all of Queen recognized a deadline. Theirs was a "shared soul". They stuck together – standing strong, aiming high, and driving themselves toward their best, right till the end. The only way they knew to defy death, depression, and despair was to keep writing, and playing, and singing. Queen, along with Mercury, had a lot of living to do before dying. When asked about Mercury's health the other members of the group either changed the subject or denied everything. They allowed little if any room for a social death to precede a physical one. Queen focused on music, producing two original albums plus a second compilation album – with the off-shoots including four more charting singles, one of which – the very long and complex "Innuendo" (1991) – hit the top spot in England immediately.

Mercury led Queen into facing death head-on, affirming life all the way. Many critics have tried to ignore the conceptual underpinnings of Queen's work, but to suggest that the many allusions to Parsi-Zarathustrian theology – generally compatible with Judeo-Christian theology – are only incidental cannot be considered a tenable conclusion. Because Queen dealt with serious moral issues long before encountering the terminal illness of its frontman, all four of the members of the group ended up far more prepared than most to handle an extended time of living with dying. Through their music they have provided members of the "Baby Boom" generation a new vocabulary for grieving. In the words of Queen's increasingly popular funeral favorite, "The Show Must Go On!"

Endnotes.

General Comments:

     (a) First, let me note some caveats. There are other places and other times in which life is or has been viewed as preparation for death. Certain faith groups hold a vision of death – and rebirth or renovation – front and center. Certain eras held a vision of death side by side with that of life. This essay considers only the general masses of those living in North America and Europe – "Judeo-Christian culture" – here and now – or at least considers that as the group against which comparisons will be made. Much of this essay concerns several individuals – one in particular – situated psychologically in a different place and time despite apparently living within modern Euro-American culture. The emphasis is twofold: (1) on the happenstance that these several individuals ended up far more prepared than most to handle an extended time of living with dying, and (2) on the impact their experience is having on helping a new generation find new words – new funeral songs – for processing grief and grieving.

     Second, let me acknowledge that, while certain themes may appear to define a life, this does not mean that the person or group living that life sat down to ponder it all. Amazingly, people write reports for school and reports for work, but rarely set aside time to write reports on themselves. Essayists of various stripes fill that gap. Much of this essay focuses on themes that are suggestive from an outside perspective and retrospective stance – a vantage point generally different from that of an individual's or group's lived experience. That is, Freddie Mercury, Brian May, Roger Taylor, and John Deacon – "Queen" – may or may not have been aware of how their lyrics were adding up to suggest the themes explored in this essay. Third, whether or not this thesis is "proved" – that for some people death is not at all "theoretical" – it is hoped that some thought-provoking points will be raised, some research paths will be suggested, and some aching hearts somewhat will be soothed. This essay is not intended to be "the last word" on living with stark medical prognosis, living with the dangers of a war-zone, the theological "meaning" of Queen, or the future of songs used for funerals.

(b) One can argue the pros and cons of spelling "G-d" with the "o" intact throughout this manuscript. The decision here has been to take the most conservative path, considering that leaving out one letter maintains the meaning while reducing the chance that a sacred name might be profaned; technically, the original guidance for taking this approach applied only within certain vulnerable areas of Hebrew writing. This manuscript attempts to be respectful to all religions mentioned and to avoid grievous misinterpretation.

[1]   Vargas JB. "Finding Grace in Facing Mortality." a frequently republished article http://www.healtharticlebank.com/Article/Finding-Grace-in-Facing-Mortality/6107 ; the quoted words first appeared in Vargas JB. The Promise of Death, The Passion of Life: A Reflective Exploration of Death, Loss, and Living Fully. Rancho Cucamonga, CA: Luminary Enterprises, 2005; p.69.

[2]   The name of the photographer could not be found, but one version of the photo has a tiny "AP" in the bottom right corner, probably standing for "Associated Press". An almost but not quite identical photo appeared on the front page of the tabloid News of the World, 24 November 1991, so apparently the photos were taken less than 24 hours before Mercury's death.

[3]   http://www.sunlifedirect.co.uk/About-Sun-Life-Direct/Press-Office/Press-Releases/Going-underground/ [both men & women chose "The Show Must Go On!" but only men chose "Bohemian Rhapsody"; 2011] http://www.queenzone.com/news/top-ten-funeral-songs.aspx "Top Ten Funeral Songs." http://funeralguide.co.za/funeral-songs/funeral songs/blog.html "Songs for Funerals." http://myfunkyfuneral.com/song.php "Your Final Sound-Track."

http://mattwalks.wordpress.com/2009/07/06/big-10-death-songs "Big 10: Death Songs" – "10. The Show Must Go On! – Queen" [July 2009] http://www.rankopedia.com/Worst-songs-to-play-at-a-funeral/Step1/15927/.htm "Worst Songs to Play at a Funeral" ["Another One Bites the Dust!" was #2; April 2009] http://www.makefive.com/categories/experiences/life/songs-for-your-funeral "Songs for Your Funeral" ["Who Wants to Live Forever?" was #9; May 2008] http://www.centralengland.coop/funeral-services/bereavement-help-and-advice/when-someone-dies/funeral-choices/funeral-music/ ["Who Wants to Live Forever?" was #11; undated page]

Brian May addressed this phenomenon somewhat in an early 2013 interview: "I suppose for some reason we seemed to be speaking about real things for real people. … all the sentiments in the songs are things that everyone feels … we spoke about the inner emotions of people. ... The emotions that we sang about are common to everybody … ." "Interview: Brian May." M Magazine / online, February 28, 2013. http://www.m-magazine.co.uk/carousel/interview-brian-may/

4   Queen. "The Show Must Go On!" (1991); it is said that Brian May primarily wrote the song, but that Freddie Mercury wrote the 1st verse while John Deacon and Roger Taylor wrote the notable chord sequences. This song and "Another One Bites the Dust!" [Duncan J. (1980)] were the two most featured on popular television programs over the last decade.

5   "Life is for the living. Death is for the dead. Let life be like music. And death a note unsaid." Hughes L. The Collected Poems of Langston Hughes. New York: Random House Digital, Inc., 1995.

6   In regard to the original name and its spelling of Queen's frontman, the most credible source found is a magazine article available on the internet: Raval S, Rana V. "The Making of a Bohemian." India Today. 1996;21:210; "There is a small entry in the records of St. Peter's High School in Panchgani, a hill resort near Mumbai: Farok Bomi Bulsara. Born: September 5. 1946." [The ancestral home, "Bulsar," now known as "Valsad," is a Gujarati city 120 miles north of Mumbai. "St. Peter's," 155

miles south of the metropolis then known as "Bombay," was until 1967 known as "The European Boys' School". Young Bulsara studied there between February 14, 1955 and February 25, 1963, ie, between ages 8 and 16. Notably, a mile east of St. Peter's is one of the few "*dakhmeh*" (burial towers) and "*aramgha*" (cemeteries) in India – as well as an "*agiari*" (fire temple) – used by those of Bulsara's faith. While the more credible account is that he finished school 2 years later back in Stone Town, Zanzibar at St. Joseph's Convent School (since 1964 known as "Tumekuja Secondary School"), the usual narrative is that he finished school at St. Mary's in Bombay's Mazgaon district. In any case, he often visited maternal grandparents and an aunt in the Dadar district, near another *agiari*, and about 5 miles north of another *dakhmeh* near Rudyard Kipling's boyhood home, "The Dean's Bungalow," at a renowned art school founded by a philanthropist also of Bulsara's faith. Jones L-A. Mercury: An Intimate Biography of Freddie Mercury. New York: Touchstone/ Simon & Schuster, 2011; pp.47-48.] As early as 23 August 1970 the name "Mercury" is known to have been on his mind as he appeared on stage in what he called his "Mercury suit" – "a black, figure-hugging, one-piece outfit" which was open to the waist to reveal his chest and on which "the ankles and wrists sported little wings"; apparently he also had a white one. Hodkinson M. Queen: The Early Years. London: Omnibus Press, 1995; Blake M. Is This the Real Life?: The Untold Story of Queen. New York: Da Capo Press, 2011 (excerpt on the web:
http://www.popmatters.com/pm/feature/137549-is-this-the-real-life-the-untold-story-of-queen/P1) While he had gone by the nickname "Freddie" for years, around 1973, after finishing writing "My Fairy King," which includes the phrase, "Mother Mercury," he legally changed his name to "Frederick Mercury" – so his passport and sheet music through at least 1985 are known to carry that name. See endnote #36 in regard to why the name "Mercury" may have been chosen.

[7]   Fonda J. from My Life So Far. NY: Random House, 2005; she credits this phrase to Fred Branfman; see
http://www.trulyalive.org/individuals/jane_fonda.htm and
http://fredbranfman.wordpress.com/about/: "created and developed the 'Life-Affirming Death Awareness' practice".

8   Seegar A. (1888-1916), "I Have a Rendezvous with Death." in Poems. New York: Charles Scribner's Sons, 1916; p.144.

9   After putting together this typology of death I found the following article, which similarly uses the variables of time and certainty: Glaser BG, Strauss AL. "Temporal Aspects of Dying as a Non-Scheduled Status Passage." Am J Sociol. 1965;71(1):48-49; p.49: "Dying is divided by medical personnel into four death expectations, which we conceive of as the transitional statuses of dying that define the patient's status passage from living to dead: (1) uncertain about death and unknown time when the question will be resolved, (2) uncertain about death and known time when the question will be resolved, (3) certain about death and unknown time when it will occur, and (4) certain about death and known time when it will occur.6 In defining which dying or transitional status the patient is in and which he is passing to, it is often far easier for the doctor to say whether or not death is certain than at what time either uncertainty will be resolved or death will occur." [ftn at the bottom of p.49:] "It is important to note the theoretical step forward that we have taken from the two articles by Fred Davis, each of which brought out the notion of differential perceptions: 'Uncertainty in Medical Prognosis,' Am J Sociol, July, 1960, pp.41-47; and 'Definitions of Time and Recovery in Paralytic Polio Convalescence,' Am J Sociol, May, 1956, pp.582-87. In the medical prognosis article, Davis discussed the differential perceptions of certainty of prognosis held by the doctor, patient, and family. In 'Definitions of Time …,' the differential perceptions of time of recovery held by these people were discussed. In our study, each participant defines the dying patient situation in terms of both certainty and time."

10   Bunyan J. The Pilgrim's Progress, Part One, Chapter 18, re "the Valley of the Shadow of Death".

11   Coyle N. "The Hard Work of Living in the Face of Death" J Pain Symptom Management. 2006 Sep;32(3):266-274. "Three subthemes emerged from the data that reflected the hard work that these individuals undertook. These were orientating themselves to the disease and maintaining control, searching for and creating a system of support and

safety, and struggling to find meaning and create a legacy. The findings confirm that living with advanced cancer in the face of death involves hard work on the part of the patient."

[12]   Inman C, Ogden J. "Facing mortality: exploring the mechanisms of positive growth and the process of recalibration." Psychol Health Med. 2011 May; 16(3):366-74.

[13]   Boswell J. The Life of Samuel Johnson. 1791; in the entry under "September 19, 1777".

[14]   Abadian S. "Cultural Healing: When Cultural Renewal is Reparative and When it is Toxic." J Aboriginal & Indigenous Community Health. 2006;4(2):5-27, p.6; the quote clearly concerns Zarathustrism, that author's faith.
http://www.pimatisiwin.com/uploads/1076630616.pdf

That author's husband made a similar point elsewhere: "surviving is not enough. … the freedom to take risks and make meaningful progress comes in part from the realization that death is inevitable. … the point is to make life meaningful while you can." [Heifetz RA, Linsky M. Leadership on the Line: Staying Alive through the Dangers of Leading. Boston: Harvard Business School Publishing, 2002; p.208]

[15]   That the members of Queen – especially May and Mercury – were singing about death "from the very beginning" is, of course, hard to prove – especially since they might not have been self-consciously aware of it at the time. At the very end of an apparently congenial interview in October 2013, May did comment as follows: "I've always been interested in death as part of life, if that makes any sense; you'll probably find that in my lyrics anyway. … Are you going to plan your life as if this is all there is, or are you going to plan it in terms of 'oh, this is the first part and the next part will be like this …'."
http://www.kerrang.com/blog/2013/10/brian_may_releases_adventures.html

That the members of Queen were singing about "various theological themes" does not make them *de jure* "men of the cloth". Much discussion has taken place about whether this or that member of Queen was or was not morally perfect. Perhaps the best response to this concern was provided on one of the music forum websites by an older woman, who commented something like this: "None of my sons or grandsons were born as 'saints' but, through trial and error, they are moving in that direction". Regardless, this essay will regard the members of Queen as *de facto* theologians.

While many have shunned the following book because of the author's obvious prejudice regarding certain people, there is no getting around the fact that this is one of the most insightful books available regarding the philosophical and theological aspects of Queen's music; chapters 6 & 7 especially are recommended: Ahundova M. The Real Story of Freddie Mercury. 2005; chapter 6; on-line ?2004? http://allofqueen.on.ufanet.ru/book/chapter6.html

[16]   See, especially, "Love Me Like There's No Tomorrow!" (1984/ 1985); note that this song title has been used at least two other times by others, and that these several songs have no relationships with each other; one can argue that Mercury's lyrics are the most elegant. For Queen's best unambiguous love ballads see, "Nevermore" (1974), "Love of My Life" (1975), "I was Born to Love You" (1985/1995), and "Golden Boy" (1987).

[17]   Abadian S. op cit.

[18]   "Keep Yourself Alive!" was the 3rd most common song on Queen's setlists, receiving especially heavy play in concert through 1984. http://www.setlist.fm/stats/songs/queen-43d6e37f.html?song=Keep+Yourself+Alive&artist=43d6e37f

Ahundova M. op cit; chapter 7 http://allofqueen.on.ufanet.ru/book/chapter7.html.

May has commented more than once that originally he meant there had to be more to living than just keeping alive. "The lyrics of 'Keep Yourself Alive' … are meant to be slightly ironical. … [They are] actually more about asking 'Is there more to life than this?'" [Brian May Interview broadcast on Absolute Radio, August 22, 2011. http://www.youtube.com/watch?v=Bz7EK41e240&feature=player_detailp age] Indeed, May appeared to be echoing Friedrich Nietzsche's Zarathustra: "Am I still alive?"– ie, "truly alive"– not "just alive"

[Nietzsche F. Thus Spoke Zarathustra: First Part (1883) "Zarathustra's Prologue," section 10; regardless of which English translation is used, the sense clearly is that just continually to "keep yourself alive" is hardly a high enough goal.] Be that as it may, the song's words meshed tightly with the theological precepts with which bandmate Mercury had been raised. Perhaps supporting the view that "Keep Yourself Alive!" might be viewed somewhat as a moral admonition is that, during Queen's tours in 1978-79, Mercury often sang part of the 1st verse of Taylor's "Fun It" (1978) as an introduction to "Keep Yourself Alive!" – the opening lines of "Fun It" being,

Everybody in the morning
should do a good turn all right.
Everybody in the night-time
should have a good time all night.

The suggestion is that one should keep alive both in order to do good and to feel good – both in order to give goodness and to receive goodness.http://www.queenpedia.com/index.php?title=The_Queen_Performance_Index

[19]   May B. "Keep Yourself Alive!" (1971).

[20]   Mercury F. "The Seven Seas of Rhye" (1974).

[21]   Mercury F. "Somebody to Love" (1976).

[22]   May B. "Dead on Time" (1978).

[23]   Deacon J. "You're My Best Friend!" (1976).

[24]   Mercury F, May B, Taylor R, Deacon J. "Soul Brother" (1981). This song, explicitly signed by all and coming at the end of their 1st decade together, intriguingly contains allusions to "Keep Yourself Alive!" (1973), "You're My Best Friend!" (1975), "Somebody to Love" (1976), "We Are the Champions!" (1977), "We Will Rock You!" (1977), and "Under Pressure" (1981) – plus a suggestion of the later appearing "Princes of the Universe" (1986).

[25]   May B. "Keep Yourself Alive!" (1971).

[26]   Mercury F. "Don't Try So Hard!" (1991).

[27]   Many sources speak of Mercury's parents as devout Parsis. One source mentions that his grandfather was a Parsi priest; (no author indicated) "The Great Pretender." Sunday London Times. 1996 November;

http://www.queenzone.com/forums/739833/sunday-times-article-about-freddies-childhood-interesting.aspx There was a well-regarded Parsi theologian and translator, Sohrab Jamshedji Bulsara (1877-1945), but whether or not he and Mercury were related is not known.

[28]   So, how widely disseminated were Queen's moralistic comments – confronting death, evil, and negativity head-on? "Don't Try Suicide!" (1980) was released as the B-side of the "Another One Bites the Dust!" (1980) single in the United States, Japan, Canada, and Australia. In the first two of those countries this specific single charted as "number one". It went on to become Queen's best-selling single EVER in the United States – carrying the anti-suicide message along with its disco beat. This is but one example – but a stunning example – of how many fans ended up with an example of Queen's moralistic commentary in their record collections. A good guess – but only a guess – is that each of these purchasing fans listened at least once to this up-tempo, bluesy anti-suicide song that had a catchy, bouncy refrain. As usual, Queen had bothered to produce a complex piece of music. The exact relationship of this song to the widely shown "public service" movie "Teenage Suicide (Don't Try It!)" (1981) has been difficult to pin down, although WorldCat ("the world's largest network of library content") includes this tag on its entry: "music composed and performed by Queen; additional music by Lee Curreri".

After writing this manuscript I discovered that a prominent Anglican clergyman, the Reverend Canon Robin Gamble – who created a stage production, "The Gospel According to Queen" – already had opined that much of Queen's music was "a cry against death, a cry for something other than mortality"
http://www.independent.co.uk/news/vicar-rocks-the-flocks-with-queen-1564455.html 19 December 1992.

[29]   Mercury F. "The March of the Black Queen" (1974).

[30]   Mercury F. "Hangman" (1972).

[31]   Mercury F. "My Fairy King" (1973).

[32]   8/8 & 12/8 "polyrhythm/ polymeter".

[33]   "The March of the Black Queen" specifically mentions "Queen of the Night" – which should have been recognized by critics as a reference to Wolfgang Amadeus Mozart's opera The Magic Flute, which portrays the morally impure queen as opposed by the morally pure "Sarastro" – that is, Zarathustra – which should have tipped off critics to look for more Zarathustrian elements in this song – especially since the song also mentions "going up to heaven and then coming back alive" – which is exactly what Zarathustra is said to have done.

[34]   for the "winged circle ring" – *faravahar* – see: http://www.persianmemories.com/sculpture/faravahar.htm

[35]   Mercury F. "The Seven Seas of Rhye" (1974).

[36]   Kipling R. The Seven Seas. London: Methuen, 1896; "experimental rhymes" and "experimental rhythms" are common contemporary comments about these poems. Not only was Kipling raised in a Parsi district of Mumbai, near where Mercury frequently visited relatives, but his beguiling "How the Rhinoceros Got His Skin" featured "a Parsee from whose hat the rays of the sun were reflected in more-than-oriental splendor" [note the seemingly gratuitous comment about "rays of the sun"] [Just So Stories for Little Children. London: Macmillan & Co., 1902], and his "A Centurion of the Thirtieth" (1906) featured "A Song to Mithras" – the representative of truth and light – the opponent of falsehood and darkness – still honored in the Parsi feast of "Mehrgān" ["Day of Meher/ Mithra"] [Puck of Pook's Hill. London: Macmillan & Co., 1906]. While Theosophists have had no problem directly identifying *Mithra* – or *Mithras* – with Mercury – both being close to the sun while serving as messengers between those in heaven and those on earth, most current academic studies appear comfortable only with noting that statues of Mercury appear quite frequently in Mithrian temples.

[37]   See "Another Live" (1975) an album by Todd Rundgren of the band "Utopia" and "The Promise" (1976) an album by Mike Pinder of the band "The Moody Blues"; both musicians wrote lyrics about "the seven rays". A photo on the web of Freddie Mercury and Todd Rundgren together in 1974 proves that they crossed paths around the time this song

was being written. It is not too far afield to suggest that these three musicians might have shared notions about "the seven rays" – and that such ideas might relate to "The Seven Seas of Rhye".

http://danielnester.com/2010/06/30/freddie-mercury-meets-todd-rundgren-c-1974/

Desborough BR. They Cast No Shadows: A Collection of Essays on the Illuminati, Revisionist History, and Suppressed Technologies. Bloomington, IN: iUniverse, 2002; p.132: "the seven Amshaspands, the first of the creative emanations of the Almighty, which correspond to the Seven Rays of Theosophy."

Palsetia JS. The Parsis of India: Preservation of Identity in Bombay City. Leiden: Brill, 2001; pp.174, 264, notes Theosophy as a mystical variant of Zarathustrism and Orthodox Zarathustrism as recognizing the "the Seven Holy Immortals" – the "Amshaspands" – "the Seven Beneficent Immortals" – the "Amesha Spentas" – as charged with guarding humans from "the endless dark" – that is, from death, negativity, and evil.

Gerard R. "Commentary." introduction to Robbins, MD. Tapestry of the Gods. The Seven Rays: An Esoteric Key to Understanding Human Nature. Volume I. Third Edition. Mariposa, CA: The University of the Seven Rays Publishing House, 1996; pp.xv-xxxvii; provides an historical overview of the place of "the seven rays" in esoteric psychology; on the web at http://pipiionline.com/downloads/Tapestry-Vol-I.pdf. Three primary classics in the field are the following: Bailey AA. A Treatise on the Seven Rays: The New Psychology. New York, Lucis Publishing Co., 1936; Hodson G. The Seven Human Temperaments. Madras, India: Theosophical Publishing House, 1952 (associates a specific individual psychological tendency to a specific given ray); Baker D. The Seven Rays: Key to the Mysteries. New York: Samuel Weiser, 1977 & Wellingborough, UK: Aquarian Press, 1977.

Zarathustrian discussions frequently refer to the number seven. For example, a core of their faith's scripture is known as Yana Haptaŋhāiti – The Seven Chapters. There also is the common Zarathustrian household phrase of "the seven c's" – referring to the "haft chin" – the seven ("haft") piles ("chin") of items – each of whose names begins with the letter "c" – set out beautifully on a ceremonial table to commemorate "Nowruz" or "Navroj" – the "New Light" – the first day of Spring. Under the Persian Achaemenid dynasty – the era of the greatest spread of Zarathustrism – this display representing the seven elements of life was called the "haft chin"; under the subsequent Arabic Umayyad dynasty it was called "haft sin". Parsi/ Zarathustrian traditionalists from Gujarat and Mumbai still refer to "the seven c's" – which would make sense if they called the table display "haft chin" – but most do this today even while using the Arabic words beginning with "s" for the seven items rather than the Persian words that begin with "c". This is just the kind of oddity that Mercury seemed to appreciate. One can easily imagine his mother talking of the holiday's "seven c's" and him responding about Kipling's book, The Seven Seas.

Having mentioned above that Zarathustrism had its greatest spread under the Achaemenids (705-675 BCE), it must be noted that during their rule Persia was described as extending to "the seven seas": the Red, Aegean, Black, Caspian, Indian, Mediterranean, and Persian bodies of water. Reflecting those times of grandeur, the premier authority on Persian words remains the Haft Qulzum – called on its title page, in English, The Seven Seas: A Dictionary and Grammar of the Persian Language (1822) – copies of which were disseminated from British India to the European capitals. The Seven Seas ... was reprinted in 1891, and its German translation of 1874 was reprinted in 1966. Anyone exploring Persian literature is bound to come across extracts from the Haft Qulzum ... .

Essentially the only non-Queen reference to "Rhye" caught by internet search engines is to the "Ernest Rhye" edition [London: J M Dent & Sons Ltd, 1935] of George Meredith's The Ordeal of Richard Feverel: A History of Father and Son (1859) – which long remained required reading in British secondary schools despite being a once tabooed psychosexual tragicomedy, whose hero is referred to as a Zoroastrian "Fire-worshipper," and whose central theme is named repeatedly as "The Magian [Zarathustrian] Conflict" between good and evil. While search engines pick up multiple associations of "Ernest Rhye" with "Richard Feverel" –

the last name "Rhye" was a typographical error; "Ernest Percival Rhys" (1859-1946) – the last name ending with an "s" not an "e" – was founding editor of the 1,000-volume, low-priced "Everyman's Library" – which, as of 1933, included Nietzsche's <u>Thus Spake Zarathustra ...</u> . If Mercury obtained that series' only two volumes relating to Zarathustrism, he may well have noted this obvious misspelling of the editor's last name – and taken this misspelling – "Rhye" for his own use. Again, this is just the kind of oddity that Mercury seemed to appreciate.

If one accepts the observation that Mercury enjoyed melodies and meters as well as plays on images and words, then there is at least one more possible explanation for the phrase "Seas of Rhye". First, consider that the first noun is plural and the second is singular; now reverse the nouns, still keeping the first noun as plural and second noun as singular, to produce "Rhyes of Sea"; now convert that newly reversed phrase into the homonymic equivalent: "Rise of C". Second, consider that there is a sizeable literature – both Christian and Zarathustrian – concerning how "the Rise of Christianity" – a very common phrase – corresponded with "the fall of Zarathustrism" – a not uncommon phrase. Third, consider that in popular writings those discussing the interactions of Christianity and Zarathustrism frequently refer to the former as "C" and the latter as "Z". That is, Mercury may have symbolically reversed the rise of Christianity – "the Rise of C" – to "the C's of Ri". Combining "the C's of Ri" with the popular Zarathustrian notion of "the Seven Seas" – meaning, to the Persians, the entire known world – which also happened to be, as noted, the title of Kipling's popular book of "melodies and meters" about Mumbai – and one has "The Seven C's of Ri" – that is, "The Seven Seas of Rhye". Reinforcing this notion of the one faith rising as the other was falling is the following: While Parsis view May 27th as marking the final earthly departure of their messenger, Zarathustra, Iranians of the faith view December 26th as the time – a date clearly colliding with December 25th – the date Christians view as marking the initial earthly arrival of their messenger, Jesus. The events would have been almost 6 centuries apart – maybe far more – but the symbolism remains, of "out with the old and in with the new". That "the new" should be honored by "the old" is represented by the notion that "the Magi" – Zarathustrian priests – made it a point to visit the new-born child – as noted in the Queen song, "Jesus" (1973): "It all began with the three wise men …". One might also recall two other messengers – the god Mercury and the god Mithra – especially since the later, too, was viewed as having arrived on December 25th.

The main point here is that it is highly unlikely that "The Seven Seas of Rhye" is a meaningless phrase – and it is very likely, given the context, that Mercury meant to comment in some way on Zarathustrism.

The larger story – somewhat complex and derived from many references – is that Zarathustrism arose in the 6th century BCE (although some suggest it arose as early as the 17th century BCE) as a "reformed" version of Mithraism, but after Zarathustra's death classical Mithraism re-emerged, overshadowing the "purer" from of Zarathustrism. Both Christianity and this mixed Mithraism/ Zarathustrism enjoyed protection in the Roman Empire during Emperor Julian's reign, from 355 to 363 CE, but only Christianity enjoyed such protection after his death. The number "seven" appears throughout the history of many religions, but Julian specifically spoke of "the seven rayed G-d". From this, "Theosophy", heavily influenced by Zarathustrism's seven "Amshaspands," developed in the late 19th century the notion of these seven "creative emanations of G-d" – or "seven rays" as being related to the seven classically observable "planets" (non-fixed observable objects in the sky) – the Sun, the Moon, Mercury, Venus, Mars, Jupiter, and Saturn – with each human's soul as being influenced by one of these seven rays – thus, "the seven rays of (esoteric) psychology". Since Freddie Mercury, nominally a Parsi – ie, an Indian Zarathustrian – and Brian May, nominally a Christian, appear to have been theologically quite compatible, and since Mercury clearly knew a lot about Christianity, having spent about ten years in Catholic schools, it is not inconceivable at all that Mercury would have known about the "parting of the ways" that the two religions were forced to take after the reign of Emperor Julian.

[38]   Mercury F. "Bohemian Rhapsody" (1975).

39   "The Path of Asha." abstracted from Taraporewala IJS. The Religion of Zarathushtra. Bombay: Chronicle Press & Madras: Theosophical Publishing House, 1926;
http://www.farvardyn.com/zoroaster2.php

40   Jobs S. "Commencement Address." 2005. Stanford University, http://news.stanford.edu/news/2005/june15/jobs-061505.html

41   Deacon J. "You're My Best Friend!" (1975).

42   Deacon J. "Spread Your Wings!" (1977).

43   Mercury F. "Keep Passing the Open Windows!" (1983).

44   Mercury F. "Mr. Bad Guy" (1985).

45   Mercury F. "Somebody to Love" (1976).

46   Mercury F. "Bohemian Rhapsody" (1975).

47   Deacon J. "I Want to Break Free!" (1984).

48   Mercury F, Taylor R. "Breakthru" (1989).

49   May B. "The Show Must Go On!" (1991).

50   May B. "Save Me!" (1979).

51   Mercury F. "Nevermore" (1974).

52   Mercury F. "Beautiful Day" (1980).

53   May B. "The Hero" (1980).

54   May B. "Flash" (1980).

55   Mercury F, May B, Taylor R, Deacon J. "Soul Brother" (1981).

56   Mercury F. "There Must Be More to Life than This!" (1983).

57   May B. "Hammer to Fall" (1984). Intriguingly, this song parallels, in theme if not tone, Mercury's "over-the-top" "The Fairy Feller's Master-Stroke" (1974) – a song that faithfully describes Richard Dadd's (1817-86) famous "over the top" painting of the same name (1855-64) depicting multitudes of observers frozen in time, waiting for the fairy feller's ominously raised ax to fall.

58   Mercury F. "It's a Hard Life!" (1984).

59   Clark D, Christie J. "Time" (1986); sung by Freddie Mercury.

60   Actually, Parsis focus on life – "Gaya"– and generally speak of "non-life" – "Aiyaiti" – rather than of "death".

61   May B. "Teo Torriatte! (Let Us Cling Together!)"

("手をとりあって") (1977).

60   Mercury F. "Love Me Like There's No Tomorrow!" (1984/1985).

63   May B. "Who Wants to Live Forever?" (1986).

64   May B. "Son and Daughter" (1973).

65   May B. "Dead on Time" (1978).

66   Clark D, Christie J. "Time" (1986).

67   Mercury is said to have been formally diagnosed as having human immunodeficiency virus in late March or early April 1987, but the speculation is that he knew during 1984 – and certainly during 1986.

68   Mercury F. "G-d is Heavy" (1984).

69   Mercury F. "Made in Heaven" (1985/1995).

70   Queen. "One Vision!" (1985); while the notion that "G-d works in mysterious ways" is commonplace enough, it occurs with notable frequency in Zarathustrian writings.

Just as the ironic aspects of "Keep Yourself Alive! (1973) and the sarcastic aspects of "Made in Heaven" (1985/ 1995) have been noted, one has to wonder about a less clear situation – whether "Don't Try So Hard!" (1991; recording finalized sometime in 1990) was not a bit "tongue in cheek". Mercury was physically ill – yet suddenly the vaguely pessimistic flow of the song is hijacked by his rejecting exclamation, "Oh, what a beautiful world! This is the life for me!" – that is, that he meant the opposite – that an accepting stance was NOT going to be the primary way he planned to live while dying. Regarding "Don't Try So Hard!" May made it clear that, "we all contributed to the creation … but … Freddie was the driving force …" behind the song. ["Stone Cold Crazy: Brian May Interview." Q Classic - March 2005.

http://www.brianmay.com/queen/tour05/interviews/bm_classicq_mar05pt1.html

71   Deacon J. "One Year of Love" (1986).

72   Deacon J. "No Turning Back" (1986). This track (the only track recorded by his band, "The Immortals") was taken seriously enough to be

reworked by Robert Ahwai for the Japanese vocalist, Minako Honda as "Roulette" (1986) – on her album, "Cancel," produced by Brian May.

[73]   May, B. "Gimme the Prize (Kurgan's Theme)" (1986); slightly supporting the view that Kurgan's intruding gruff voice might be significant is the fact that this song was re-released 1998 as the "B side" of May's "No One But You (Only The Good Die Young)" (1997); compare the tentatively defiant *"It's better to burn out 'cause rust never sleeps,"* in Neil Young's "Hey Hey, My My (Into the Black)" (1979), and the blatantly defiant *"it's better to burn out, yeah, than fade away,"* in Def Leppard's "Rock of Ages" (1983); "Kurgan's words" re-appeared in the last lines of musician Kurt Cobain's suicide note (1994). Compare also that in "Khashoggi's Ship" (1989) the narrator (Mercury?) sings, *"The best years of my life are like a supernova"* – that is, like an extremely bright but brief burst of light – with almost no fading away involved.

[74]   Deacon J. "Friends Will Be Friends" (1986).

[75]   Squirer B. "Love Is the Hero" (1986); arranged by Freddie Mercury, who also wrote and sang the opening words.

[76]   Mercury F, Moran M. "La Japonaise" (1987).

[77]   Mercury F, Moran M. "Barcelona" (1987). While many know of the "Mercury Phoenix Trust" [for research and education on acquired immune deficiency syndrome ("AIDS")], that was launched with the proceeds from "A Concert for Life: The Freddie Mercury Tribute Concert for AIDS Awareness" (20 April 1992), fewer are aware that Mercury and Caballé donated the proceeds from this recorded single to the Institut Pasteur (Paris) for AID research. [Gilson G. "An Opera Legend in Athens" {interview of Caballé}. Athens News. 31 Aug 2012, pp.12 & 29; http://www.athensnews.gr/issue/13511/57936]

[78]   Mercury F, Moran M. "Ensueño" (1987); Montserrat Caballé wrote the lyrics – and this possibly was the first time the famous soprano had written lyrics; the original wordless aria had been titled, "Exercises in Free Love" (1987).

[79]   Ram B. "The Great Pretender" (1955); cover by Freddie Mercury in 1987.

[80]   Deacon J. "My Life Has Been Saved!" (1987).

[81]   Mercury F, Moran M. "How Can I Go On?" (1987).

[82]   May B. "Headlong!" (1991).

[83]   Mercury F, Taylor R. "Innuendo" (1991).

[84]   May B. "Nothin' But Blue" (1992) [Cozy Powell (1947-98) co-authored the music]; Mercury F, Taylor R. "Innuendo" (1991). The notion of "Living or dying, we'll just keep on fighting!" also got played out in two spontaneous jam-session songs recorded back-to-back in 1989, "Party" and "Khashoggi's Ship," where the resigned last lines of the one:

> Goodbye, goodbye, goodbye goodbye –
> the party is over!

are wiped away by the defiant first lines of the immediately following second:

> Who said that
> my party was all over? ...
> I'm in pretty good shape!

[85]   Casandra, in Euripides (480-406 BCE), <u>The Trojan Women</u>, lines 401-2.

[86]   May B. "Scandal!" (1989). Queen's 13th album, "The Miracle," recorded during the year after Mercury told his bandmates the extent of the illness, was, until the last moment, titled after one of its songs: "The Invisible Man" (1989), by Taylor – which includes the line,

> No-one knows what I've been through.

[87]   Queen. "Hang On In There!" (1989). Re "Hang On In There": No one seems to have noticed that Mercury's idol, Aretha Franklin, filled a song with this phrase – over and over and over: "Mr. D.J. (5 For The D.J.)" (1975):

> ... Hang on in there – and let it rock!
> Oh, hang on in there – and let it roll! ...
> Hang on in there – Good G-d almighty!
> Hang on in there – you gotta
> shake your funky soul! ...

[88]   Taylor R. "These are the Days of Our Lives" (1990).

[89] May B, Mercury F. "Bijou" (1991).

[90] The phrase appears in the Judeo-Christian psalms – most memorably in the 23rd Psalm: "Surely righteousness and mercy will follow us all the days of our lives" – that is, "forever". It also appears in the common translations of Maimonides' Sefer Hamitzvot or Book of Commandments: "We have six mitzvot which are perpetual and constant, applicable at all times, all the days of our lives" – that is, "forever".

[91] Queen. "One Vision!" (1985).

[92] Taylor R. "A Kind of Magic" (1986).

[93] Mercury F. "All G-d's People" (1987/ 1991); a demo version titled "Africa by Night" was recorded in 1987. The lines

So all you people,
give freely! ...
Don't turn your back on
the lesson of the Lord!

echo a recurrent phrase that appeared two decades earlier in Mercury's "Mad the Swine" (1991):

So all you people,
gather around!
Hold out your hands and
praise the Lord!

These latter lines were recorded in 1972 but the song was not released until the same year "All G-d's People" was released – which may or may not be a coincidence. The phrase, "all G-d's people" also appears in the complex song "The Miracle" (1989), said to have been written primarily by Mercury and Deacon.

[94] Mercury F. "A Winter's Tale" (1991/1995).

[95] May B. "Mother Love" (1991/1995).

[96] May B. "The White Queen (As It Began)." (1974).

[97] May B. "Nothin' But Blue" (1992); with this second line clearly echoing Freddie Mercury, "We Are the Champions" (1977). While the song was released after Mercury's death, the lyrics were written the eve before. " 'Nothin' But Blue' was written 'the night before Freddie died. I

had this strong feeling that it was going to happen. It flowed out very quickly. I could just hear the song in my head'." [interview]. "Brian May wants to rock you. Guitarist accepts Queen history but seeks acclaim for solo effort." Orange County Register. 04 Apr 1993.
http://www.queenarchives.com/index.php?title=Brian_May_-_04-04-1993_-_The_Orange_County_Register

[98]   May B. "Dear Friends" (1974).

[99]   Goffin G, King C. "Goin' Back" (1966); cover by Freddie Mercury in 1973 under the name "Larry Lurex". Queen. "One Vision" (1985).

[100]   Deacon J. "No Turning Back" (1986); Queen. "Hang On In There!" 1989; Mercury F. "We Are the Champions!" (1977); May B. "Nothin' But Blue." (1992).

[101]   Mercury F. "Love Me Like There's No Tomorrow!" (1984/1985).

[102]   Taylor R. "These Are the Days of Our Lives" (1991).

[103]   Deacon J. "No Turning Back" (1986); Queen. "Hang On In There!" (1989).

[104]   May B. "Nothin' But Blue" (1992).

[105]   May B. "The Show Must Go On!" (1991).

[106]   Mercury F, Taylor R. "Innuendo" (1991).

[107]   Mercury F. "Life Is Real" (1982); Clark D, Christie J. "Time" (1986).

#

Addendum – for the 2nd edition.

The author, as an historian, considers it important that the original pagination of a published text be maintained, so that citations already published will remain accurate. Thus, these corrections and augmentations have been provided in an addendum rather than having been placed within the original text. Perhaps the most valuable addition has been an index.

Corrections to Endnotes

Endnote 2 should be changed. The photo is from "Tragic Face of Freddie Mercury," The Sun (UK), 29 April 1991, page 1.

In the original endnotes, the one coming after endnote 61 and before endnote 63, obviously, should be endnote 62, but it was printed erroneously as a second endnote 60.

Additions to Endnotes

General Comment:

The following additions are numbered according to the numbers assigned to the original endnotes, but with an asterisk added after each superscript number.

3*   "Top 10 Death Songs List & Best Songs about Dying," New Movies List, 23 August 2015, included "Hammer to Fall" as number 9 on the first list and "The Show Must Go On!" as number 10 on the second.

Re "The Show Must Go On!": "It's a long story, that song, but I always felt it would be important because we were dealing with things that were hard to talk about at the time, but in the world of music you could do it." May B. interview. Guitarist Magazine, October 01, 1994. http://www.queenarchives.com/index.php?title=Brian_May_-_10-01-1994_-_Guitarist_Magazine

6*   Since 1964 the political entity "Zanzibar," a former British protectorate, has become part of The United Republic of Tanzania, on the East African country's largest island portion, Unguja (itself sometimes simply called "Zanzibar"). Mercury always identified himself as "British".

15*   Now at https://www.wattpad.com/457068809-the-history-of-freddie-mercury-by-mv-ahundova-page

28*   Not only was "Don't Try Suicide!" (1980) widely disseminated as the B-side of Queen's most sold single in the United States, it also appeared on Queen's most sold studio album in the United States, The Game (1980), which included two "number one" hits. https://medium.com/cuepoint/the-game-how-queen-conquered-and-lost-america-a3c48103ac62

At least one other investigator also has asked how widely played was "Don't Try Suicide!" His widely-sold paperback noted that the song "gained considerable airplay on rock radio when DJs tired of playing its A-side ["Another One Bites the Dust!"]".
Purvis G. Queen: The Complete Works. London, Reynolds & Hearn, 2006; un-numbered pages under the alphabetized entry "Don't Try Suicide!"

A number of reviews focused on the song's intriguing bass line and piano work; that is, the song was noted as much for its music as for its message. Fans did listen to it. The "verses are bluesy, the chorus is catchy rock, [and] the bridge and the solo have great rockabilly feel ..."
http://www.queensongs.info/song-analysis/songwriting-analyses/modern-era-queen/the-game/don-t-try-suicide

Just as "Don't Try Suicide!" was the B-side of a number-one single – and thus received heavy distribution, "Keep Passing the Open Windows!" – Queen's other anti-suicide song – was the B-side of "Thank G-d It's Christmas!" (1984) – a natural for seasonal sales and one of the few songs – rock or not – acknowledging that not everyone enters the holiday season feeling happy. The opening lines of the three verses are:

Oh, my love, we've had our share of tears ....
The moon and stars seem awful cold and bright ....
Oh, my love, we've lived in troubled days ....

The refrain, of course, is

Thank G-d it's Christmas!

Further addressing the question of how widely disseminated were Queen's moralistic comments is the fact that, for two decades, the name of Queen's first single has graced the title of a widely distributed mental health manual, Keep Yourself Alive: Prevention of Suicide in Young People ... [Martin G, Clark S, Beckinsale P, Skene C, Stacey K. Adelaide, Australia: Foundation Studios, 1997].
http://familyconcernpublishing.com.au/wp-content/uploads/2014/01/KYA.pdf

30*   Regarding the writing of "Hangman": "According to another private collector, who asked Brian about this song in the early 1990s, a letter exists where Brian confirms that Freddie wrote the lyrics and Brian wrote the music." http://www.queenpedia.com/index.php?title=Hangman

38*   The startling line in "Bohemian Rhapsody" (1975) – "Mama, 'just killed a man" – had been preceded by Mercury's "Killer Queen" (1974), but Taylor orchestrated another play on words, producing, so to speak, a "Queen Killer," when, in 1977, he got the group to commission artist Frank Kelly Freas (1922-2005) to modify his existing magazine cover art – of a chagrined robot who accidentally "killed a man" – into arresting rock album cover art – of a mournful robot who accidentally "killed the band". [The album does include May's "All Dead, All Dead" (1977).] The

original art, for a novella by Tom Godwin (1915-1980) – "The Gulf Between" (Astounding Science Fiction, October 1953) – was about the astonishing gulf between humans and robots. Numerous web commentators have noted how, when they were children, this cover art for Queen's sixth studio album, News of the World (1977), both scared and fascinated them. Indeed, an alternative cover, featuring the accidentally-killing robot but not the accidentally-killed band members, was used by some retailers, notably, K-Mart. The television program "Family Guy" focused on all this in an episode, "Killer Queen," aired in early 2012.
https://www.facebook.com/QueenThroughTheYearsAPhotographicHistory/photos/a.177382672423194.1073741829.177370252424436/366522093509250/
https://en.wikipedia.org/wiki/News_of_the_World_(album)
http://coverlovers.quora.com/Queen-News-of-the-World
http://www.brianmay.com/queen/queennews/queennewsmar12a.html
https://www.youtube.com/watch?v=9V_CvrkSnaQ
https://www.youtube.com/watch?time_continue=200&v=fxQHi1QXboo

May's question, "Is there more to life than this?" echoes, of course, the song written by Mercury, "There Must Be More to Life than This" (1981), released in 1985, later finally re-released as a duet with Michael Jackson (2014) years after the original collaboration. The song even asserts, "There must be more to life than living".

51*   The notion of "not living in my life" – of becoming dead – contained in "Nevermore" (1974) also is reflected in the last lines of "The March of the Black Queen" (1974):

> *But now it's time to be gone!*
> *La la la la forever forever!*
> *Ah ah ah ah ah!*

The notion of being "gone forever" – of becoming dead.

60*   While the original text notes that songs "somehow relating to death and its defiance" make up "a fifth of those released in the two decades by the *members* [italics added] of Queen," they actually make up over a third of the songs released specifically under Queen's name.

63*   Regarding the notion of "Who Wants to Live Forever?": "...if you examine the tenets of Zoroastrianism ... then you will find that they state that earthy life is a temporary condition wherein the believer must deal with the struggle between truth and falsehood. This is not to say that when the believer dies, [he or she] ... will be reincarnated; rather, [his or her] ... soul is returned to the protection of [his or her] ... guardian spirit, or *fravashi*. Even then, in the spiritual world, the soul is expected to continue the battle between what is true and what is not. There is not the calm acceptance of mortality that one finds in Buddhism; the expectation here is that there is always more work to do, more battles to fight. You might 'live forever,' even if you don't particularly savour the prospect." Carlin M, Friese F. "Queen: A Kind of Magic." Then Play Long, 27 August 2014; http://nobilliards.blogspot.com/2014_08_01_archive.html .

That is, just as Jews are commanded to perform mitzvah – gut-level acts of justice and mercy – but are provided little if any guidance as to what to do, Zarathustrians are commanded to "keep yourself alive" – to "live forever" – both in this world and in the next – so as to continue fighting – whether they want to or not –

> evil ["the not true"],
>
> negativity ["the not positive"], and
>
> death ["the non-life," "the endless dark," "the gone forever"]

Like the Jewish lament, "Who Wants to Be the Chosen People?" the Zarathustrian lament is "Who Wants to Live Forever?" In each case the impulsive answer might be along the lines of, "no one in his or her right mind" – but such is the commandment.

"Who Wants to Live Forever?" (1986) was re-recorded in 1989 on behalf of the British Bone Marrow Donor Appeal, raising £150,000 for treatment of childhood leukemia. May, who produced the track, played guitar and keyboard; Taylor played drums; Deacon played bass; definitely tear-jerking vocals were provided by two child performers, Ian Meeson and Belinda Gillet. Toward being a bit more hopeful, the last lines were changed from

Forever is our today.
Who waits forever
anyway?

to

Forever is ours. We
only need a chance
to live.

"Rock star aids charity's last act." BBC News, 7 June 2005;
http://news.bbc.co.uk/2/hi/uk_news/wales/4616535.stm
http://www.ultimatequeen.co.uk/queen/songs/collaborations.htm#
https://www.youtube.com/watch?v=XnGF3xj2U6I

Further regarding the relationship of this question, "Who Wants to Live Forever?" to the question of immortality, apparently Zarathustra/ Zoroaster himself was among those attracted to the possibility of eternal life – and a clarification about immortality therefore was incorporated into Zarathustrian theology.

> We are informed that when Zoroaster asked for immortality from G-d, the latter replied that if Zoroaster were to remain immortal, the wicked Turbaratur would also remain immortal, [and that] the resurrection would then be impossible and mankind without hope.

[Geiger W, Spiegel F. The Age of the Avesta and Zoroaster; translated into English by Sanjānā DDP; London, H. Frowde, 1886; p.125.]

Also consider the following more recent comment:

> … the only thing everlasting is "the undying quest for excellence". In the Zoroastrian sacred poetry, Immortality is about triumph of the spirit over limitations, and cosmic development into godhood. Mortal men are not doomed to a dismal death in the realm of shadows, instead earthlings are destined to live with the Immortal Gods as god-men, and their faith is to arise, go beyond, overcome themselves and excel. … Partaking of the nectar of immortality means to overcome, and evolve ever higher and better.

66

[Ardeshir {clearly a *non de plume*}. "Immortality and the eternal quest for excellence." Authentic Gatha Zoroastrianism; "the blog site of the Orthodox Zoroastrianism Yahoo Group"; 2016 Aug 4; https://authenticgathazoroastrianism.org/2016/08/04/immortality-and-the-eternal-quest-for-excellence/

65*   When "Dead on Time" appeared as a single (rather than as an album track) in 1979, the versions issued in Germany, Spain, and Bolivia carried "Mustapha" (1978) on the A-side – that is, as the primary song. A reasonable question is, "Why?"

"Mustapha," with its Arabic and Arabic-sounding phrases, served as the first track of Queen's seventh studio album, Jazz (1978), and its opening lines –

Ibrahim! Ibrahim! Ibrahim!
Allah, Allah, Allah, Allah will pray for you!

– were used to introduce performances of "Bohemian Rhapsody" (1975) during 1979, as well as of "Hammer to Fall" (1984) during 1985. That is, "Mustapha" was not a throw-away song and these were not throw-away lines. Again, "Why?" Some sources erroneously use the more conventional phrasing: "Allah, *we'll* pray for you," but the official website, www.queenonline.com , makes it clear that the phrasing indeed is: "*Allah will* pray for you!" There is quite a literature on this notion of G-d praying to G-d on mortals' behalf. Apparently, when it comes to the question of "For what does Allah/ G-d pray?" both Jewish and Muslim scholars come up with essentially the same answer: the deity prays that the deity's mercy will conquer the deity's anger – that the deity's compassion will go beyond the bounds of strict justice. [Christian mortals have Jesus, Mary, and the saints to intercede for them.] Thus, the invocation precedes the questionable behaviors portrayed in "Bohemian Rhapsody," "Hammer to Fall," and in the next five tracks of Jazz. [see "Berachot 7a," in Talmud; http://blog.webyeshiva.org/does-god-pray-aggada-insight-by-rabbi-yitzchak-blau/ ; and, "Book 4, Volume 54, Hadith 416," in Sahih Bukhari: http://www.hadithgarden.com/2010/12/allah-wrote-in-his-book-my-mercy.html ; the current author could not find any specific Zarathustrian reference to prayer by the deity to the deity on mortals' behalf.]

[67*] While it seems doubtful that Mercury had any definitive knowledge in 1986 about having acquired immune deficiency syndrome ("AIDS"), at least one tabloid had no problem speculating about this. Whitow H. "Do I Look Like I'm Dying of AIDS? Fumes Freddie," The Sun (UK), 18 October 1986, p.1.

[69*] Regarding the question of whether Mercury was or was not being sarcastic with the lyrics of "Made in Heaven" (1985) – it is notable that the video accompanying the song certainly suggests a scene out of hell rather than out of heaven. Indeed, Mercury clearly meant to reference Dante's Inferno and Igor Stravinsky's most famous work – The Rites of Spring {Le Sacre du printemps} (1913) (which Stravinsky composed in Montreaux, Switzerland – the home of Queen's recording studio). The Rites of Spring, originally choreographed and danced by Vaslav Nijinsky (1890-1950), concerned a pagan ritual in which a sacrificial virgin dances herself to death – a scene which might well be viewed as out of hell rather than out of heaven. Mercury, one year earlier, in part of Deacon's "I Want to Break Free!" (1984), had recreated Nijinsky's scandalous portrayal in The Afternoon of a Faun {L'après-midi d'un faune} (1912) of an erotic rural god blatantly ignoring social propriety – that is, of someone "breaking free". Clearly, both Nijinski and up-ending convention were on Mercury's mind.
Gunn J, Jenkins J. Queen: As It Began. London: Sidgwick & Jackson, 1992; pp.237-238.

[81*] Mercury's *ad lib* lines recorded live in concert in 1989 –
  I'm in no doubt.
  I'm blind.
  I don't know what's coming to me.
– indeed do not appear on the "Queen Official" version of the song posted on YouTube.

[82*] The image of frantically rushing "Headlong!" – a song recorded almost exactly one year before Mercury's death – certainly suggested the

insistent progression of his illness. While one might rush headlong into the future, or into marriage, or into happiness, overall the image tends to suggest rushing into a risky situation – into something less positive – even into death. That the single of "Headlong!" was released in early 1991 with "Mad the Swine" – a song recorded in 1971 but never released before 1991 – as its "B side" – somewhat confirms this line of thinking. The Biblical story – written down three times – in the books of Matthew, Mark, and Luke – concerns mad swine rushing headlong to their death in the sea. The modern computer-based literal translation of the original Greek texts uses the word "headlong" each time. This is not to say that the meaning of either "Mad the Swine" or the Biblical story is crystal clear. https://bible.knowing-jesus.com/words/Headlong/type/leb/sort/popular

87*   Freddie Mercury's "Somebody to Love!" (1976) obviously pays homage to the gospel music sound of Aretha Franklin. In 1989, Mercury actually commented, "with Aretha, I'd do something, sort of, gospelly, 'cause ... we have done, you know with Queen, sort of gospel overtones. I mean, 'Somebody to Love' had that .... I'd love Aretha to sing 'Somebody to Love', actually. That would be a nice thing, if somebody approached her and said 'try that'. But, um, no I mean, I mean, trying to sing with her, um, I don't know, she hasn't approached me yet." "Queen for An Hour." Interview. Radio 1, May 29, 1989. http://www.ultimatequeen.co.uk/queen/miscellaneous/queen-for-an-hour-radio-1-interview.htm

92*   "Who Wants to Live Forever?" (1986), "One Year of Love" (1986), "Gimme the Prize (Kurgan's Theme)" (1986), "A Kind of Magic" (1986) [all four noted above] as well as Mercury's "Princes of the Universe" (1986) were written between early September 1985 and late January 1986 for "Highlander" (1986) – a movie clearly focused on the theme of good versus evil – a project demonstrating that all four members were signed on at the same time to the twin notions of "facing death head-on" and of "affirming life while fully aware of death". The specifically Zarathustrian theme was not acknowledged in the movie but was acknowledged in the subsequent television series that began airing in 1997.

Beberg AL. "1. Highlander: The Movie (There Can Be Only One)." in The Unofficial Highlander WWW and List Archive Site. published on the web, 1994-2016.

A notable oddity of the line "who wants to live forever?" is that it was spoken in the Queen-scored movie "Flash Gordon" (1980) six years before the song "Who Wants to Live Forever?" was written by Brian May for "Highlander". One has to wonder if that line spoken in the earlier movie had connected in some special way with May, such that it stayed on his mind all those years. [May B. "Battle Theme" {instrumental; superimposed movie dialogue written by Lorenzo Semple, Jr}, track 13, Flash Gordon.

94*   Regarding Zarathustrian end-of-life customs:
"Preparing for One's Demise.
The focus of an individual ... when preparing for ... demise is three-fold. First, to be serene and at peace with oneself – *armaiti*. The second, is to conclude preparations for the soul's afterlife. The third, is one's legacy – a passing of the spiritual flame, and where possible, a tangible legacy of service to the community. These steps contribute to a person accepting the inevitability of mortality and a realization that while mortal life is short, spiritual life will exist till the end of time." Eduljee KE. "After Life & Funeral Customs." in Zoroastrian Heritage. book published on the web, 2005-2014.
http://heritageinstitute.com/zoroastrianism/death/index.htm
Certainly, "to be serene and at peace" seems to have been the goal of Mercury's "A Winter's Tale" (1991/1995).

A fair amount of confusion has existed regarding the exact timings of Mercury's performances of "A Winter's Tale" and of "Mother Love". As best can be sorted out, the vocals of the first were recorded on May 10, 1991, and the vocals of the second were recorded on May 22, 1991 – as deduced from the discovered track-sheets. In other words, the "not that many weeks before dying" phrase has been stretched out a bit. Shirley-Smith J. blog entry, "Freddie's Final Vocal Confirmed (?)". Queen Zone, December 04, 2013.

http://www.queenzone.com/forums/1364363/freddies-final-vocal-confirmed.aspx

[97*]   The lyrics of "Nothin' But Blue" definitely are May's, but apparently the instrumental version, with less guitar and without lyrics – titled "Somewhere in Time" (1992) – should be credited to Cozy Powell, Geoff Nicholls and Steve Makin; on that version, May did play guitar and John Deacon did play bass.

http://www.ultimatequeen.co.uk/queen/songs/collaborations.htm#SomewhereInTime

[105*]   "Inside my heart is breaking…, but my smile … stays on!" See, Khosro Khazai [= "Khosro Khazai Pardis"]. "A Journey through the Zoroastrian Experience"; this was a lecture delivered in 2008; currently it is available on the web as part of the Sydney Studies in Religion at https://openjournals.library.sydney.edu.au/index.php/SSR/article/view/683/664 ; p.5. "these important and highly symbolic words, told and repeated through the century about Zarathustra 'who was born with a smile, lived with a smile and died with a smile'. In this context Pliny, the Roman naturalist of the first century, could write that Zarathustra was the first child to be born with a smile on his lips. … This legend but powerful symbol is one among many others which indicate the joyful way of *Arta* ['the right' or 'the true'; 'harmony'; cf *Asha*]."

Many Queen fans and scholars will think immediately of Brian May's earlier band, "Smile" – but that band was formed and named in 1968 – before May met Freddie Bulsara. See also endnote 18 above re May's possible early acquaintance with Zarathustrian notions.

Index – for the 2nd edition.

kill, killed, killer – 14, 17, 39,63-
64
"Kind of Magic, A," see, "A
Kind of Magic"
Kipling R – 17, 44, 50, 52-53
"Kurgan's Theme," see, "Gimme
the Prize (Kurgan's
Theme)"

(l)
"La Japonaise" – 30, 34, 57
lame, see also, "illness,"
"immune," & "sarcoma"
– 37
"Let Us Cling Together!" see
"Teo Torriatte!"
life, live, living, alive, see also,
"Gaya" – the entries
cover almost every page
"Life Is Real" – 2, 60
light-hearted – 8, 19
light of life – 6
lists – 3, 12, 25, 47
Lord, see also, "G-d" – 20, 31,
35, 59
love, loved, lovers, loving,
lovingly – 9, 11-12, 15-
16, 20, 22-23, 25-26, 29-
30, 34, 36, 38, 47-48, 55-
57, 59-60, 63, 68-69,
74,76
"Love Is the Hero" – 30, 57
"Love Me Like There's No
Tomorrow!" – 25-26, 38,
47, 56, 60

(m)
"Made in Heaven" – 27, 56, 68
"Mad the Swine" 59
Magi, Magian, magic – 35-36,
50, 52, 54, 59, 65, 69,
72, 76
"Magic Flute," see "The Magic
Flute"
Maimonides – 59
maintain, maintained,
maintaining, maintains –
11, 14, 22, 42, 45, 61
"March of the Black Queen," see
"The March of the Black
Queen"
May B – 4, 13, 41, 43, 46, 47,
48, 54, 55, 56, 57, 58,
59, 60, 62, 63, 64, 68,
69, 71
Mazda – 13, 72
medical, see also "health" – 42,
45
Meeson I – 65
Meher, Mehrgān, see also
"Mithra" – 50
melodically, melodies, melody –
15, 17, 21, 26, 53
Mercury F – the entries cover
almost every page
"Mercury," origin of the name –
44
Mercury Phoenix Trust – 57
"Mercury suit" – 44
Mercury (the god) – 53-54

77

Meredith G – 52

messenger, messengers – 50, 53-54

meter, meters – 16-17, 49, 53

Michael Jackson, see "Jackson M"

millionaire, see "The Millionaire Waltz"

miracle – 21, 58-59

Mithra, Mithraism, Mithras, Mithrian – 13, 22, 50, 54

mitzvah, mitzvoth – 59, 65

Montserrat Caballé, see "Caballé M"

moral, moralistic, morality, morally – 8, 14, 18, 36, 40, 47-50, 63

Moran M – 31, 57-58

mortal, mortality, mortals – 9, 22, 42, 46, 49, 51, 56, 65-67, 70, 74

mother (Mercury's) -- 52

"Mother Love" – 36, 59, 70

"Mother Mercury" – 44

Mozart WA – 50

"Mr. Bad Guy" – 20, 55

"Mr. D.J. (5 For the D.J.)"

Mumbai – 17, 43, 50, 52, 53

Muslim – 67

"Mustapha" – 67

"My Fairy King" – 15, 44, 49

"My Life Has Been Saved!" – 31, 33, 57

mysteries, mysterious, mystical – 17, 28, 51, 56

(n)

Navroj – 52

negative, negativity – 12, 14, 16, 17, 23, 49, 51, 65

never – [2], 18, 21, 30, 39, 47, 55, 57, 64

"Nevermore" – 21, 47, 55, 64

New Light – 52

Nietzsche F – 47, 48, 53

Nijinsky V – 68

"non-life, the," see also, "Aiyaiti," "death," "endless dark," "gone forever," & "not living" – 55, 65

"No One But You (Only the Good Die Young)" – 57

"Nothin' But Blue" – 58-60, 71

"not living," see also, Aiyaiti, "death," "endless dark," "gone forever," "non-life"– 64

"not true, the," see also "evil – 65

"not positive, the," see also "negativity" – 65

"No Turning Back" – 29, 39, 56, 60

Nowruz – 52

(o)

oddity, see also "ironic" & "sarcasm" – 52-53, 69

Ogden J – 46

79

About the Author

Robert Charles Powell, MD, PhD

After earning a bachelor's degree in the natural sciences, with special distinction in the social sciences, from Shimer College (Illinois), a "Great Books" school, he earned doctorates in medicine and in philosophy from Duke University (North Carolina), within its Behavioral Sciences Study (linguistic psychiatry & theoretical biology) and Medical Historian Training (European/ American history of science & of ideas) programs. His earliest writings concerned the development of holistic/ organismic theory in psychosomatic medicine, the concept of the subliminal/ subconscious, and the invention of clinical pastoral chaplaincy. Following postgraduate work at the SUNY/ Upstate Medical Center (Syracuse) (psychiatry/ neurology/ medicine), and at the Michael Reese Institute for Psychosomatic & Psychiatric Research (Chicago) (clinical research on adolescence), he earned certification by the American Board of Psychiatry & Neurology. He taught briefly at the medical schools of the University of Missouri – Kansas City, the University of Wisconsin – Milwaukee, and Northwestern University. His earliest research coordination concerned lithium and premenstrual syndrome.

Having earlier hitch-hiked throughout the British Isles, France, and Italy, he was among the last solo travelers on the overland trail from Istanbul to Kabul to Katmandu – eventually wandering throughout Iran, India, Thailand, and Myanmar (Burma).

In private practice for 34 years, he generally treated mixed psychiatric/ neurologic/ endocrinologic disorders in all age groups. During much of that time, he also worked, as a civilian medical officer, with military active duty personnel, retirees, and dependents, on whatever problems with which they presented, without assuming these to have emotional etiology. With sustained curiosity, he explored, among other things, how non-psychiatric factors masquerade as psychiatric disorders, how inflammatory factors impact the whole body (including the brain), and how answers to five short questions can suggest a person's level of ego organization.

He and his wife, Pat, have a blended family of two sons and one daughter. In November 2013, they moved from the Chicago Northshore to the Long Island Northshore. In October 2016, they moved to the northwest suburbs of Boston, to be closer to their children and grandchildren.

His most popular booklet is Anton T. Boisen (1876-1965): "Breaking an Opening in the Wall between Religion and Medicine," 1976. His 2nd most popular booklet is C.P.E. [Clinical Pastoral Education]: Fifty Years of Learning, through Supervised Encounter with "Living Human Documents," 1975.

His most popular article is "Helen Flanders Dunbar (1902-1959) and a Holistic Approach to Psychosomatic Problems. I. The Rise and Fall of a Medical Philosophy," Psychiatric Quarterly 49: 133 -152, 1977; available online through ResearchGate. His 2nd most popular article is "The 'Subliminal' versus the 'Subconscious' in the American Acceptance of Psychoanalysis, 1906-1910," Journal of the History of the Behavioral Sciences 15: 155-165, 1979; revised & updated as a chapter in Freudian Concepts in America: The Role of Psychical Research in Preparing the Way: 1904-1934, 2015. An article he most wishes had wider availability is "Psychosomatic Aspects of Affect in Psychoanalytic Theory, 1950-1970," invited review essay, The American Academy of Psychoanalysis Forum 23 (4): 5-8, 1979.   #

Also by

Robert Charles Powell

Available through
Amazon, Kindle, and
other fine booksellers

PENTOXIFYLLINE
:
A VERSATILE
OFF-PATENT MEDICINE
BEST NOT OVERLOOKED
:
*Overview with
Extensive Bibliography*

FREUDIAN
CONCEPTS IN
AMERICA
:
THE ROLE OF
PSYCHICAL RESEARCH IN
PREPARING THE WAY
:
1904-1934

LISTENING
CLOSELY TO
PATIENTS
WITHOUT
JUMPING TO CONCLUSIONS

*"You Don't Have to Be
Brilliant.
You Just Have to Be
Curious."*

Made in the USA
Middletown, DE
06 January 2019